What Comes Down to Us

What Comes Down to Us

25
Contemporary
Kentucky
Poets

Edited by
Jeff Worley

Foreword by
Ed McClanahan

The University Press
of Kentucky

Scholarly publisher for the Commonwealth,
serving Bellarmine University, Berea College, Centre
College of Kentucky, Eastern Kentucky University,
The Filson Historical Society, Georgetown College,
Kentucky Historical Society, Kentucky State University,
Morehead State University, Murray State University,
Northern Kentucky University, Transylvania University,
University of Kentucky, University of Louisville,
and Western Kentucky University.
All rights reserved.

Editorial and Sales Offices: The University Press of Kentucky
663 South Limestone Street, Lexington, Kentucky 40508-4008
www.kentuckypress.com

13 12 11 10 09   5 4 3 2 1

LIBRARY OF CONGRESS CATALOGING-IN-PUBLICATION DATA

What comes down to us : 25 contemporary Kentucky poets /
edited by Jeff Worley.
p. cm.
Includes bibliographical references and index.
ISBN 978-0-8131-2557-2 (hardcover : alk. paper)
1. American poetry—Kentucky.   2. American poetry—20th century.
3. Kentucky—Poetry.   I. Worley, Jeff, 1947–
PS558.K4W47 2009
811'.540809769—dc22
2009020810

To Kentucky poets—past, present, and future

CONTENTS

FOREWORD

My friend and fellow Kentuckian Wendell Berry spent part of the 1968–1969 school year teaching creative writing at Stanford University, in the same department in which I was, at the time, clinging like a burdock stick-tight to an untenured lectureship that, if I'd managed to hang onto it, would have transplanted me forever in the meager, hostile soil of California, where I'd have been approximately as indigenous as an artichoke in a Kentucky tobacco patch.

In April 1970, about a year after Wendell had returned to his farm in his native Henry County, Kentucky, he wrote me a letter, which included this passage:

> I think the crisis of my life was the discovery that I was a
> Henry County poet, a kind of creature that, so far as I knew,
> had no precedent in creation, and that I feared was contrary to
> evolutionary law. I think I went around for years suspicioning
> that I was the sole member of an otherwise non-existent species.
> It was like I began with one foot on the ground, very uncer-
> tainly balanced, and all my work has been the slow descent of
> the other foot. Now I think the other foot has come all the way
> down and planted itself in Henry County along with its mate.
> ... [W]hen a Henry County poet begins at last to see himself as
> one of the natural possibilities of Henry County, and not as an
> evolutionary accident, then he quits worrying so much about
> getting stomped out, and begins going around, grinning, saying
> over and over to himself: "I am possible. I am possible."*

Although the twenty-five poets whose work graces this splendid collection have obviously experienced Kentucky in twenty-five utterly various ways, I'd venture to say that at some "I am possible" moment of personal epiphany, every one of them has, like Wendell, planted that other foot firmly on the ground and declared to himself or herself, "Whatever else I may have been or might yet become, I am a *Kentucky* poet."

Yet for all their patriotic attachment to our beloved, much abused "place on earth" (to borrow one more phrase from Wendell), there is not a single local colorist or rustic versemonger among them, not one parochial syllable in all the poems gathered here. These poets speak from every corner of the state—from the Appalachian Mountains to a Henry County tobacco patch to a sweaty gymnasium in Louisville to a sonorous cavern in the depths of Mammoth Cave—and their voices are heard around the world.

Great poetry is that rare natural resource which, by definition, can't be exploited or exhausted, and so Kentucky's abundance of it is, for once, not a curse but a blessing. Jeff Worley's collection is a treasure that enriches us forever, and its publication is an occasion for celebration and rejoicing.

Ed McClanahan
Author of *Famous People I Have Known* and *O the Clear Moment*

For the full text of Wendell's letter, along with the poem that accompanied it, see Spit in the Ocean #7: All About Kesey, *ed. Ed McClanahan (New York: Viking-Penguin, 2003).*

INTRODUCTION

In corresponding with a New York literary agent several years ago, Kentucky poet James Baker Hall found this question scrawled across the bottom of a letter: "How come there are so many good writers working now in Kentucky?" The literary agent might have been wondering: Is it something in the water? Something in the bourbon?

It's a good question, which I posed to two Kentucky-born poets.

Eastern Kentucky writer George Ella Lyon believes that the answer might lie in Kentucky's historical and geographical sense of place. "It seems to me a lot of forces intersect in Kentucky. East and west, north and south. We've been seen as Frontier and as Backwater, traditional and renegade. We've got mountains and rivers, flatlands and bluegrass; we're landlocked yet water-bordered. We were 'neutral' during the Civil War, yet both Lincoln and Davis were born here." She says all of these factors give rise to writers trying to make sense of these various connections through their art.

"Accounting for Kentucky's vibrant literary tradition, especially poetry, is like trying to analyze what makes a delicious burgoo," says Richard Taylor. "Was it the Big Boy tomatoes, the added rabbit, cooking time, container, seasoning, the proportions of vegetables to meat, the wood heat? Maybe our writerly tradition grows from the fact that Kentucky is a place where people know who they are and who their people were, a relatively homogeneous population with an accessible past that has both richness and a darker hue."

In her 2007 speech in Frankfort, Jane Gentry, Kentucky's newly inducted poet laureate, focused on the importance of narrative, which, she said, has always been front and center in the state's poetic consciousness. "Kentucky is a state full of storytelling, and has been since before it was a state, when it was the first American frontier, the new Eden, in the eighteenth century. The first Kentuckians were adventurers, who left the comforts of settled homes to come to a dangerous, promising wilderness. To adventure, to self-challenge, to journeys into the unknown, story is a natural and inevitable response."

It's obvious to anyone who pays attention to serious literature in this country that contemporary Kentucky prose writers, in particular, have established national and international reputations: Bobbie Ann Mason, Sena Jeter Naslund, Ed McClanahan, Barbara Kingsolver, Chris Offutt, Chris Holbrook, Gurney Norman, Kim Edwards, and Wendell Berry, to name a few. One purpose of this anthology is to bring more recognition to talented Kentucky poets who keep the burgoo simmering.

Anthologies are, by their very nature, selective: they are appetizers, not entrees. At their best, these collections whet a reader's appetite for more, for a book—or several—by the newly discovered author. Anthologies provide readers with a useful shortcut to the fuller works of writers, and in this way these collections are important and useful, especially, I would argue, for younger readers.

Anthologizing Kentucky poets is not a new idea. In the past forty-five years, several collections have brought Kentucky poets together. In 1964, Joy Bale Boone, a great promoter of poetry and poets in the state, and Kentucky poet laureate from 1997 to 1998, edited a collection titled *Contemporary Kentucky Poetry,* which was published by Friends of Kentucky Libraries. She included poems by thirty-eight poets, Jesse Stuart being the only "name" poet in this group. This collection had a limited press run and sold out in a few months. Three years later, *Kentucky Harvest,* edited by David Brandenburg, was published. He included sixty poets, though nearly all (Jim Wayne Miller is an exception) wrote verse, truth be told, rather than poetry.

In 1976 Jonathan Greene's Gnomon Press gave us *Kentucky Renaissance: An Anthology of Contemporary Writing,* a handsome publication that included both fiction and poetry. In 1990, four friends, two of them University of Kentucky students, founded Lexington Press and published *Through the Gap: An Anthology of Contemporary Kentucky Poets*. The initial press run sold out almost immediately, according to coeditor Marguerite Floyd. Two years later, White Fields Press in Louisville published *The Dark Woods I Cross: An Anthology of Contemporary Louisville Women Poets*. This special issue of the short-lived *Thinker Review* brought together thirty-nine Louisville poets. And in 1999 Elizabeth Oakes and Jane Olmstead edited *Writing Who We Are: Poems by Kentucky Feminists,* which was published through Western Kentucky University.

Most recently, the University Press of Kentucky in 2005 published a literary omnibus edited by Wade Hall titled *The Kentucky Anthology: Two Hundred Years of Writing in the Bluegrass,* which features a whopping 179 writers of fiction, poetry, essays, journals, books, and plays. The writers included range from John James Audubon to Abraham Lincoln, James Still to Hunter S. Thompson. The last section in this collection, "A Shower of Poets: Contemporary Kentucky Poetry," is a snapshot of poetry being written in our state today, each poet typically represented by one or two poems.

My goal with *What Comes Down to Us*—the title comes from a line by Davis McCombs, the youngest poet represented here—is to bring together a more generous sampling of poems written by our state's most accomplished and best-known writers, to showcase the diversity and richness of poems being written right now in Kentucky. This anthology brings together twenty-five poets whose subjects range from love to joy to death, to the vicissitudes of childhood and adolescence, to relationships with friends, siblings, parents, and lovers, to our tenuous and enduring place in history. In other words, the themes that have always attracted and intrigued poets.

To the charge that this is a regional collection, I plead guilty. But American literature has always been rooted in the regional, rooted in particular places and times. A region's best writers have consistently explored the richness of their own immediate surroundings for the insightful and necessary links between the local and the universal.

My selection criteria were as follows. The poets must have published at least two collections (including chapbooks), and no self-published books were considered. In selecting poets for the anthology, I was most interested in writers who have an active literary presence in the state; who regularly give readings and other public presentations or workshops; whose poetry has been honored with local, state, and/or national awards; and who place poems regularly in local and national literary magazines. Excellence was the only criterion I used in selecting the poems.

And finally, the writer must be a Kentucky poet.

But just what is a "Kentucky poet"? Someone, for starters, who writes poems, if not compulsively, then often and diligently as a matter of habit. The poets in this book have an exemplary record of publications, readings, and awards. They have won Al Smith awards, National Endowment for the Arts fellowships, Guggenheim fellowships, and other prestigious honors. Four of the poets included here have served as Kentucky poet laureate, and all of the writers here share a combination of sureness of technique, depth of feeling, and a sense of commitment to language and experience.

But what makes these poets distinctively *Kentucky* poets? My answer: because they have chosen to live here and write here, and to be associated in a literary context with the state. They are comfortable wearing the mantle of "Kentucky writer."

All of the poets included—those born here and those of us who are "adopted Kentuckians," to use a phrase from Joy Bale Boone—have made Kentucky a matter of allegiance. They identify themselves and are identified as Kentucky poets. Twenty of the twenty-five are current Kentucky residents, and the other poets included return often to Kentucky in their poems.

The verbal consciousness of the poets featured here has, at least in part, been formed by their living in Kentucky. There is something about our state that has attracted the eye and ear and sensibilities of all these poets, from the unique quality of light playing over the grass where thoroughbreds play to signature geographical features like Central Kentucky's rock fences. Familiar sensory images abound in these poems, making us know we're at home:

> a nameless black mason whose
> gnarled hands, palms worn
> to the pink, could size a rock
> and slap up each day 16 feet
> of fence that was "horse high,
> bull strong, and pig tight,"
> ("Notes for a Manual on Form," Richard Taylor)

> The tobacco stands over me
> breathing as I breathe,
> its exhaling full of sweet narcotic.
> ("Alpheus Waters, July 13, 1882," Joe Survant)

> . . . We stood in the hot circle
> of her breath, stroking her long, sleek nose,
> warming our hands. We breathed in the hay-
> barn scent of her skin. We ran our palms
> over her withers, a broad smooth run
> like a ski-trail high on a mountain ridge
> ("Homeward," Frederick Smock)

These images help define the poets as Kentucky writers. But as James Baker Hall says in one of his poems, "Light is the special grace / to be sure, but the effects are our own" ["Monet"]. These effects are the accumulations of images and lines that result from practiced poetic skill and a simple receptiveness to the language as it plays itself out on the page.

Despite an occasional nod to traditional forms—Berry, for example, employs patterned end rhyme and rhymed couplets in two poems here—the poets in this collection favor the long-standing convention of free verse, or what might more usefully be called "discovered form." This term, coined by critic Charles O. Hartman in *Free Verse: An Essay on Prosody,* implies both invention and revelation, and "represents an experience shared by the reader and the poet through the poet's mimetic representative, the speaker." Although the events that happen during poetic composition can only be guessed at by even an alert reader, a good poem embodies an immediate sense of these events. The best poems share this sense of excitement of discovery as the poet moves from line to line toward some closure that doesn't suggest itself until the poet arrives there.

The poets are presented here chronologically, and a brief biography follows each poet's contribution. Compiling the work of these poets has been a wonderfully enriching experience. This project led me to read or reread nearly a hundred books, to delight in spending time with poems both familiar and new, to say to myself (in some instances), Why haven't I heard more from *this* poet before?—when he or she pulls off some particularly difficult sleight of hand or voice.

I'm grateful for the writers here who have delighted me, and I'm happy that the University Press of Kentucky has chosen to bring this collection to readers who will also find pleasure in these pages. Because, finally, these poems belong to the reader. Here's hoping they will take you somewhere new, somewhere memorable, and that you will return to them often.

I would like to express my thanks:

To the poets of Kentucky, for writing such engaging and memorable poems, and delighting me for many fine evenings as I made my way through the selection process.

To the presses, for granting permission to reprint these poems, as chronicled in the poem credits section at the end of this book. May this anthology encourage readers to seek out and buy the poets' individual collections.

To the University Press of Kentucky, for shepherding me through the tricky process of publishing an anthology, especially Stephen Wrinn, Laura Sutton, Ila McEntire, Melinda Wirkus, Ann Malcolm, and Mack McCormick. I appreciate their commitment to publishing the excellent contemporary literature of our state.

And to others—friends and poets and unofficial therapists—who have helped. You know what you did, and you have my gratitude: Richard Taylor, Marcia Hurlow, Mike Courtney, Michael McFee, Morris Grubb, Paul Zimmer, and Ed McClanahan. And to my wife, Linda, a large smooch for her excellent editorial suggestions.

WENDELL
Berry

b. 1934

The Man Born to Farming

The grower of trees, the gardener, the man born to farming,
whose hands reach into the ground and sprout,
to him the soil is a divine drug. He enters into death
yearly, and comes back rejoicing. He has seen the light lie down
in the dung heap, and rise again in the corn.
His thought passes along the row ends like a mole.
What miraculous seed has he swallowed
that the unending sentence of his love flows out of his mouth
like a vine clinging in the sunlight, and like water
descending in the dark?

Burley Coulter's Song for Kate Helen Branch

The rugs were rolled back to the wall,
The band in place, the lamps all lit.
We talked and laughed a little bit
And then obeyed the caller's call—
Light-footed, happy, half entranced—
To balance, swing, and promenade.
Do you remember how we danced
And how the fiddler played?

About midnight we left the crowd
And wandered out to take a stroll.
We heard the treefrogs and the owl;
Nearby the creek was running loud.
The good dark held us as we chanced
The joy we two together made,
Remembering how we'd whirled and pranced
And how the fiddler played.

That night is many years ago
And gone, and still I see you clear,
Clear as the lamplight in your hair.
The old time comes around me now,
And I remember how you glanced
At me, and how we stepped and swayed.
I can't forget the way we danced,
The way the fiddler played.

Rising

for Kevin Flood

1.

Having danced until nearly
time to get up, I went on
in the harvest, half lame
with weariness. And he
took no notice, and made
no mention of my distress.
He went ahead, assuming
that I would follow. I followed,
dizzy, half blind, bitter
with sweat in the hot light.
He never turned his head,
a man well known by his back
in those fields in those days.
He led me through long rows
of misery, moving like a dancer
ahead of me, so elated
he was, and able, filled
with desire for the ground's growth.
We came finally to the high
still heat of four o'clock,
a long time before sleep.
And then he stood by me
and looked at me as I worked,
just looked, so that my own head
uttered his judgment, even
his laughter. He only said:
"That social life don't get
down the row, does it, boy?"

2.

I worked by will then, he
by desire. What was ordeal
for me, for him was order
and grace, ideal and real.

That was my awkward boyhood,
the time of his mastery.
He troubled me to become
what I had not thought to be.

3.

The boy must learn the man
whose life does not travel
along any road, toward
any other place,
but is a journey back and forth
in rows, and in the rounds
of years. His journey's end
is no place of ease, but the farm
itself, the place day labor
starts from, journeys in,
returns to: the fields
whose past and potency are one.

4.

And that is our story,
not of time, but the forever
returning events of light,
ancient knowledge seeking
its new minds. The man at dawn
in spring of the year,

going to the fields,
visionary of seed and desire,
is timeless as a star.

5.
Any man's death could end the story:
his mourners, having accompanied him
to the grave through all he knew,
turn back, leaving him complete.

But this is not the story of a life.
It is the story of lives, knit together,
overlapping in succession, rising
again from grave after grave.

For those who depart from it, bearing it
in their minds, the grave is a beginning.
It has weighted the earth with sudden
new gravity, the enrichment of pain.

There is a grave, too, in each
survivor. By it, the dead one lives.
He enters us, a broken blade,
sharp, clear as a lens or a mirror.

And he comes into us helpless, tender
as the newborn enter the world. Great
is the burden of our care. We must be true
to ourselves. How else will he know us?

Like a wound, grief receives him.
Like graves, we heal over, and yet keep

as part of ourselves the severe gift.
By grief, more inward than darkness,

the dead become the intelligence of life.
Where the tree falls the forest rises.
There is nowhere to stand but in absence,
no life but in the fateful light.

6.
Ended, a story is history;
it is in time, with time
lost. But if a man's life
continue in another man,
then the flesh will rhyme
its part in immortal song.
By absence, he comes again.

There is a kinship of the fields
that gives to the living the breath
of the dead. The earth
opened in the spring, opens
in all springs. Nameless,
ancient, many-lived, we reach
through ages with the seed.

Come Forth

I dreamed of my father when he was old.
We went to see some horses in a field;
they were sorrels, as red almost as blood,
the light gold on their shoulders and haunches.
Though they came to us, all a-tremble
with curiosity and snorty with caution,
they had never known bridle or harness.
My father walked among them, admiring,
for he was a knower of horses, and these were fine.

He leaned on a cane and dragged his feet
along the ground in hurried little steps
so that I called to him to take care, take care,
as the horses stamped and frolicked around him.
But while I warned, he seized the mane
of the nearest one. "It'll be all right,"
he said, and then from his broken stance
he leapt astride, and sat lithe and straight
and strong in the sun's unshadowed excellence.

Her First Calf

Her fate seizes her and brings her
down. She is heavy with it. It
wrings her. The great weight
is heaved out of her. It eases.
She moves into what she has become,
sure in her fate now
as a fish free in the current.
She turns to the calf who has broken
out of the womb's water and its veil.
He breathes. She licks his wet hair.
He gathers his legs under him
and rises. He stands, and his legs
wobble. After the months
of his pursuit of her, now
they meet face to face.
From the beginnings of the world
his arrival and her welcome
have been prepared. They have always
known each other.

To the Unseeable Animal

My daughter: "I hope there's an animal
somewhere that nobody has ever seen.
And I hope nobody ever sees it."

Being, whose flesh dissolves
at our glance, knower
of the secret sums and measures,
you are always here,
dwelling in the oldest sycamores,
visiting the faithful springs
when they are dark and the foxes
have crept to their edges.
I have come upon pools
in streams, places overgrown
with the woods' shadow,
where I knew you had rested,
watching the little fish
hang still in the flow;
as I approached they seemed
particles of your clear mind
disappearing among the rocks.
I have waked deep in the woods
in the early morning, sure
that while I slept
your gaze passed over me.
That we do not know you
is your perfection
and our hope. The darkness
keeps us near you.

The Peace of Wild Things

When despair for the world grows in me
and I wake in the night at the least sound
in fear of what my life and my children's lives may be,
I go and lie down where the wood drake
rests in his beauty on the water, and the great heron feeds.
I come into the peace of wild things
who do not tax their lives with forethought
of grief. I come into the presence of still water.
And I feel above me the day-blind stars
waiting with their light. For a time
I rest in the grace of the world, and am free.

III   Look Out

Come to the window, look out, and see
the valley turning green in remembrance
of all springs past and to come, the woods
perfecting with immortal patience
the leaves that are the work of all of time,
the sycamore whose white limbs shed
the history of a man's life with their old bark,
the river under the morning's breath quivering
like the touched skin of a horse, and you will see
also the shadow cast upon it by fire, the war
that lights its way by burning the earth.

Come to your windows, people of the world,
look out at whatever you see wherever you are,
and you will see dancing upon it that shadow.
You will see that your place, wherever it is,
your house, your garden, your shop, your forest, your farm,
bears the shadow of its destruction by war
which is the economy of greed which is plunder
which is the economy of wrath which is fire.
The Lords of War sell the earth to buy fire,
they sell the water and air of life to buy fire.
They are little men grown great by willingness
to drive whatever exists into its perfect absence.
Their intention to destroy any place is solidly founded
upon their willingness to destroy every place.

Every household of the world is at their mercy,
the households of the farmer and the otter and the owl
are at their mercy. They have no mercy.
Having hate, they can have no mercy.
Their greed is the hatred of mercy.
Their pockets jingle with the small change of the poor.
Their power is their willingness to destroy
everything for knowledge which is money
which is power which is victory
which is ashes sown by the wind.

Leave your windows and go out, people of the world,
go into the streets, go into the fields, go into the woods
and along the streams. Go together, go alone.
Say no to the Lords of War which is Money
which is Fire. Say no by saying yes
to the air, to the earth, to the trees,
yes to the grasses, to the rivers, to the birds
and the animals and every living thing, yes
to the small houses, yes to the children. Yes.

from *Sabbaths 2003*

Three Elegiac Poems

Harry Erdman Perry, 1881–1965

I

Let him escape hospital and doctor,
    the manners and odors of strange places,
    the dispassionate skills of experts.

Let him go free of tubes and needles,
    public corridors, the surgical white
    of life dwindled to poor pain.

Foreseeing the possibility of life without
    possibility of joy, let him give it up.

Let him die in one of the old rooms
    of his living, no stranger near him.

Let him go in peace out of the bodies
    of his life—
    flesh and marriage and household.

From the wide vision of his own windows
    let him go out of sight; and the final

time and light of his life's place be
    last seen before his eyes' slow
    opening in the earth.

Let him go like one familiar with the way
        into the wooded and tracked and
        furrowed hill, his body.

II

I stand at the cistern in front of the old barn
in the darkness, in the dead of winter,
the night strangely warm, the wind blowing,
rattling an unlatched door.
I draw the cold water up out of the ground, and drink.

At the house the light is still waiting.
An old man I have loved all my life is dying
in his bed there. He is going
slowly down from himself.
In final obedience to his life, he follows
his body out of our knowing.
Only his hands, quiet on the sheet, keep
a painful resemblance to what they no longer are.

III

He goes free of the earth.
The sun of his last day sets
clear in the sweetness of his liberty.

The earth recovers from his dying,
the hallow of his life remaining
in all his death leaves.

Radiances know him. Grown lighter
than breath, he is set free
in our remembering. Grown brighter

than vision, he goes dark
into the life of the hill
that holds his peace.

He is hidden among all that is,
and cannot be lost.

Testament

And now to the Abyss I pass
Of that Unfathomable Grass . . .

1.

Dear relatives and friends, when my last breath
Grows large and free in air, don't call it death—
A word to enrich the undertaker and inspire
His surly art of imitating life; conspire
Against him. Say that my body cannot now
Be improved upon; it has no fault to show
To the sly cosmetician. Say that my flesh
Has a perfection in compliance with the grass
Truer than any it could have striven for.
You will recognize the earth in me, as before
I wished to know it in myself: my earth
That has been my care and faithful charge from birth,
And toward which all my sorrows were surely bound,
And all my hopes. Say that I have found
A good solution, and am on my way
To the roots. And say I have left my native clay
At last, to be a traveler; that too will be so.
Traveler to where? Say you don't know.

2.

But do not let your ignorance
Of my spirit's whereabouts dismay
You, or overwhelm your thoughts.
Be careful not to say

Anything too final. Whatever
Is unsure is possible, and life is bigger
Than flesh. Beyond reach of thought
Let imagination figure

Your hope. That will be generous
To me and to yourselves. Why settle
For some know-it-all's despair
When the dead may dance to the fiddle

Hereafter, for all anybody knows?
And remember that the Heavenly soil
Need not be too rich to please
One who was happy in Port Royal.

I may be already heading back,
A new and better man, toward
That town. The thought's unreasonable,
But so is life, thank the Lord!

3.
So treat me, even dead,
As a man who has a place
To go, and something to do.
Don't muck up my face

With wax and powder and rouge
As one would prettify
An unalterable fact
To give bitterness the lie.

Admit the native earth
My body is and will be,
Admit its freedom and
Its changeability.

Dress me in the clothes
I wore in the day's round.
Lay me in a wooden box.
Put the box in the ground.

4.
Beneath this stone a Berry is planted
In his home land, as he wanted.

He has come to the gathering of his kin,
Among whom some were worthy men,

Farmers mostly, who lived by hand,
But one was a cobbler from Ireland,

Another played the eternal fool
By riding on a circus mule

To be remembered in grateful laughter
Longer than the rest. After

Doing what they had to do
They are at ease here. Let all of you

Who yet for pain find force and voice
Look on their peace, and rejoice.

VI

for Jonathan Williams

The yellow-throated warbler, the highest remotest voice
of this place, sings in the tops of the tallest sycamores,
but one day he came twice to the railing of my porch
where I sat at work above the river. He was too close
to see with binoculars. Only the naked eye could take him in,
a bird more beautiful than every picture of himself,
more beautiful than himself killed and preserved
by the most skilled taxidermist, more beautiful
than any human mind, so small and inexact,
could hope ever to remember. My mind became
beautiful by the sight of him. He had the beauty only
of himself alive in the only moment of his life.
He had upon him like a light the whole
beauty of the living world that never dies.

from *Sabbaths 2003*

One of our country's most venerated writers, **Wendell Berry** is the author of more than fifty collections of poems, novels, short stories, and essays. He was born in Henry County, Kentucky, where both sides of his family have farmed for at least five generations. In 1960, Berry published his first novel, *Nathan Coulter,* which began his chronicle of fictional Port William, a small village on the Kentucky River based on Port Royal, his hometown.

Berry earned a B.A. and M.A. in English at the University of Kentucky, and in 1958 attended Stanford University's creative writing program, thanks to a Wallace Stegner Fellowship. He studied under Stegner in a seminar that included Larry McMurtry, Edward Abbey, and Ken Kesey. From 1962 to 1964, he taught English at New York University's University College in the Bronx, and from 1964 to 1977 and 1987 to 1993 taught creative writing, nonfiction, and literature courses at the University of Kentucky. Berry's many awards include a Guggenheim Fellowship, a Rockefeller Fellowship, the T. S. Eliot Award, a 2000 Poets' Prize for *The Selected Poems of Wendell Berry,* and the Thomas Merton Award.

As a prominent defender of and spokesman for agrarian values, Berry espouses what he refers to as "the good life," which includes sustainable agriculture, healthy rural communities, connection to place, the pleasures of husbandry and good work, support of the local economy, reverence, and the interconnectedness of life. In his work, Berry challenges the threats to this good life, which include industrial farming and the industrialization of life, ignorance, hubris, greed, and violence against others and against the natural world.

For Berry, poetry lives "at the center of a complex reminding," underscoring for both the poet and the reader the poem's crafted language, its formal literary antecedents, "the formal integrity of other works, creatures and structures of the world."

On "Look Out," Berry says: "Some would call this poem a 'protest poem.' Any such poem I write is held answerable to a few rules I follow more or less consciously—though how successfully I can't say:

1. Make the poem a satisfactory pattern of sounds.
2. Make it rhythmically coherent.
3. Make the lines begin and end right.
4. Make every line, every word, count.
5. Make line and syntax interact strongly.
6. Begin at the beginning, end at the end.

I don't try to 'think up' poems or niggle them into existence. After all, nobody has hired me to be a poet. Inspiration matters to me, and I wait to be inspired. If a poem is to be any good, it needs to announce itself somehow as a possibility, and I get into its drift and work hard to make it good. In addition to being answerable to the rules above, 'Look Out' was written also to avoid the sin of silence in the presence of a public wrong."

JAMES
Baker
Hall

1935–2009

Item One in a General Theory of Things

for Barry Spacks

I remember a scene from *The Sophomore*:
Harry Zissel happens to be across
the street from a big city phone company
at 5:30 when the operators & secretaries
get off.

All of a sudden the building
opens up and out pours a jackpot of women
in their summer dresses, 400–500 of them,
it's beautiful.

Sometimes I think the whole
world has turned into a phone company
at 5:30. Sometimes I can hardly remember
seeing a man for days.

What's happened
to all the men? If I thought the rest
of them would disappear, and leave me
here, it would be one thing, but I can't
think men don't amount to anything anymore
without thinking less of myself.

I can't
walk to work anymore without falling
in love three or four times.

It's exhausting!
Where are all these women coming from?
I've got other things to do—

It Felt So Good but Many Times I Cried

depending on how brave I was
I would leave the cedar closet door open
sometimes only a crack
as little as possible
I would have to stop halfway in
waiting for my eyes to adjust
once I took off my pajamas
at that juncture usually I waited
in order to touch the fox
first you had to go into its face and ask permission
then you had to take its yellow eyes to the door
to the crack only when it knew where it was
were you free to run your hands up and down
the whole length of its fur your fingers spread
and to turn your hand over letting the wrist drag
to take the whole piece up to your face to smell it
or more exactly smell mother
I took that piece
into the darkest corner
her piece we called it
we got down into our own little place
just the two of us between coats sometimes
my blue eyes its yellow
among the dresses
I took off my clothes
I rubbed the red fox
and its missing body
into mine this limb then that
it felt so good but often I cried
I kissed its nose its eyes

I may even have stuck my tongue inside its mouth
rubbing fur back and forth across my face
over my eyelids many times over my eyelids
it felt so good but often I cried
and when I was ready I mounted it rode it
mother's fur was there right there
its missing body was there
entering mine and many other things
as well entering me it felt so good
but many times I cried

The Buffalo

crossing the yard to the old wall
I'm drawn along a circle
through each thing a full moon
seen over a considerable area of the earth
including the vast oceans rises
and walks down the wall
and through me
in the evolving white shape of a cat
for years these stones lay afield
gathering his footsteps even the clicks
sound old and have come a long way
his fur slipping through my hands
what did my ancestor hear
upon seeing the Shawnee step into
this moonlight with a small stone taken up
and shaped to his use what did the Shawnee hear
when the gun was cocked where did the sounds go
when the buffalo were slaughtered
were they fixed in time
or were they freed
into the real world mistaken
for snapping twigs or distant
thunder or history at night
when the small creatures walk this wall
isn't it the same gravity audible
the weight of each thing settling
defining the size of its earth the dead
clicking along in the moonlight with us
great silences in between
and within each of them

the dwindling herds
thundering back and forth
far and then farther away
the dwindling gunshots and screams
we shot them from trains for sport
we ate their tongues

Welcoming the Season's First Insects

Each with its own language, contingencies,
catalogues, instructions. When I imagine
all the creatures living within me,
within one cell of me,

I become a sun. All the midges
hanging over all the meadows

swarm within me, becoming one sound.
I sit here like a wishbone
in the garden's late light,

early spring, the sun's
tuning fork. The ants

ornament my skin in a line. Small
by reason of the great distance
between them and my eye

they carry me off. The weight
of their feet

sings, bless us,
we've made it
this far.

Ridge Owl Black Dog

Willie is old his face white
the white crawls up his forehead
and over his ears nowadays whenever
he lifts his tired white face up off
the floor it's to say
this may be the last time
you guys show a little feeling
I say do you want to go out
directing the question to the white
on white surrounding his eyes
like an owl's
   At the sound
of the O word Willie's
old nozzle hits the floor
his head retreats into his shoulders
his imploring eyes feature cataracts
and self-pity
    It's painful for him
to stand any more more an adventure
than he wants to undertake getting over the sill
and down the one flagstone step
     a large
plain yellow dog mostly lab a field creature
the main dog for years headlong through tall grass
through thickets fearless with the neighboring pitbull
Nowdays he moves only to stay close indoors only
occasionally does his bark sound familiar
When the owl of the ridge woods gets going
The rest of the time he's deaf
His nails stiff-legging it along behind

you over the hardwood at feed time
can break your heart
            Last night
in the middle of the night I
heard them in a dream in the dream they
were clicking in circles around
the hollow house trying
to remember something themselves
to begin with maybe the owl
maybe a way back to Mary Ann
And echoing
            The sound
of his heavy hobbling nails
on hardwood slipping
every few steps was the same
in the dream as in waking life
except the hobble had nothing to follow was wandering
from room to hollow room and then back
No master no friends
No owl of the ridge
Not even a trace

Jake the monster black dog
who's come to live here
despite everything we can do
lies curled up in the leaves
or under a bush out one door or another
sometimes on Willie's backporch cushion

We don't feed the monster
We don't make over him
We treat Jake like he's not here

Still the owl up on the ridge there
won't get going won't even check in
Maybe the owl on the ridge up there
isn't up there any longer
that's what the dream
seems to me to be about
how Jake's presence changes everything
Where the cats will agree to be fed
Whether we can lure Willie
out the door for his business
I tell myself to wake up
I say Willie needs you
He's lost he's lost it
But I stay asleep until
the sound of his loose bowels hits
the floor and wall in the front room

Thick shitty blood that's what I think
he's slipped and fallen into thrashing about
in the half-light from the hallway
                              I think
the seizure tracking him for months
has finally caught up and grabbed him
                              My hand
to his quivering head helps him hold on
                    Mary Ann
I cry out

            Together we quiet him and clean him up
as best we can inside the house the floor and walls
as best we can at night
            Come morning
we hose him down out back and towel him

which entails facing the nemesis Jake
who gets one long whiff of Willie's quiver
and at nightfall disappears that's exactly
what he did

      Where is the big black dog
who's not coiled up in the leaves
or under a dark bush with Willie
asleep at my feet again
And the ridge owl back
with its O sounds egg-
like alliterations deep-
throated and feathery

Is he off getting fed
Is he on his way back

For Mary Ann

       I'll ring you up
I'll say dearest
You'll answer
with that laugh

Don't quit laughing
There'd be no counting the people
jerked headlong into grief

Here's the boogie deal
I keep ringing you up
You keep picking up the call

Former poet laureate of Kentucky **James Baker Hall** published eight books of poetry, the most recent being *The Total Light Process: New and Selected Poems,* two novels, and many short stories. He was also a well respected and award-winning photographer who published five books of photographs, including *Tobacco Harvest: An Elegy* and *A Spring-Fed Pond.* He exhibited his photographs widely and for many years was a contributing editor for *Aperture.*

Hall's poems appeared in the most prestigious magazines and periodicals in the country, including the *Paris Review,* the *Hudson Review,* the *New Yorker,* the *Sewanee Review, Poetry,* the *American Poetry Review,* and the *Kenyon Review.* He won numerous awards, including a National Endowment for the Arts Fellowship, an Al Smith Fellowship from the Kentucky Arts Council, a National Endowment for the Arts Southern Arts Fellowship in photography, a Pushcart Prize for poetry, and an O. Henry Award for fiction. He twice served as a judge for the Pulitzer Prize in poetry.

Hall, a Lexington native, said that at age nineteen he was "snatched away from the world of sports, girls, and cars" and into his lifelong devotion to art by T. S. Eliot's "The Love Song of J. Alfred Prufrock," where "I heard for the first time the sound of a loosened tongue, and began to understand that I'd been raised to keep my mouth shut." He graduated from the University of Kentucky in 1957, having studied writing under the poet Robert Hazel alongside fellow students and future lifelong friends Wendell Berry, Ed McClanahan, and Gurney Norman. In 1960 he received a Stegner Fellowship at Stanford University, where he earned a master's degree in English.

Hall taught at Stanford, New York University, the University of Connecticut, and the Massachusetts Institute of Technology before returning to Kentucky in 1973, where for twenty-five years he directed the writing program at the University of Kentucky. A renowned and influential teacher at UK, he received the prestigious Chancellor's Award for Excellence in Teaching. He lived in Harrison County with his wife, Mary Ann Taylor-Hall, the author of three books, including the novel *Come and Go, Molly Snow.*

On writing his first poems, Hall said: "During the late '60s and early '70s, I taught fiction writing and photography at MIT. In the spring of 1969, Denise Levertov, one of the most respected poets in the country, came to MIT to teach a poetry workshop. With cross-registration from other nearby schools, the course was way over-subscribed, and I was asked to teach the overflow. I hadn't written poetry since I was an undergraduate, and this was in the middle of the counterculture, in a place where all authority was under challenge. I had to start writing poetry in order to maintain my credibility as the workshop teacher."

Hall died June 25, 2009, at his home near Sadieville, Kentucky, after a long illness.

JANE
Gentry

b. 1941

A Garden in Kentucky

Under the fluorescent sun
inside the Kroger, it is always
southern California. Hard avocados
rot as they ripen from the center out.
Tomatoes granulate inside their hides.
But by the parking lot, a six-tree orchard
frames a cottage where winter has set in.

Pork fat seasons these rooms.
The wood range spits and hisses,
limbers the oilcloth on the table
where an old man and an old woman
draw the quarter-moons of their nails,
shadowed still with dirt,
across the legends of seed catalogues.

Each morning he milks the only goat
inside the limits of Versailles. She feeds
a rooster that wakes up all the neighbors.
Through dark afternoons and into night
they study the roses' velvet mouths
and the apples' bright skins
that crack at the first bite.

When thaw comes, the man turns up
the sod and, on its underside, ciphers
roots and worms. The sun like an angel
beats its wings above their grubbing.
Evenings on the viny porch they rock,
discussing clouds, the chance of rain.
Husks in the dark dirt fatten and burst.

Taking the Train from Maysville to New York

September 11, 2002

Leaving Versailles at 4 a.m., only a glint of light
in the east. The stars so quiet. One watching
above the gable of my house, close as in childhood.
On the drive to Maysville, just a handful of cars
on the country highways. Out the window I see
the gauze of the Milky Way unrolled across the sky.
The Dipper so clear, dot to dot. Orion lazy, low
to the horizon. Near Paris, the sheerest sliver
of the new moon raises the old above the trees.

Then on the train headed toward West Virginia,
running alongside the broad-bosomed Ohio,
the levee now gold in the rising sun,
farmsteads, entire cities of rolled hay,
power plants with smoke plumes blooming
into the pink sky, towns of vine-latticed houses
facing the tracks. Oh for the voice of Whitman
or Twain to catalog these visions of America
framed by the train window, much as they lay
150 years ago. Through the dappled
trees yellowed in sun, I see the mist, the lovely
breath of the Ohio rising in shafts, alive, inviting
rest, but my sleep-heavy eyes won't close out
the sun blazing its pathway on the river.

The rails sing a low, syncopated song.
The coach cradles me and rocks across small rivers
and large, past cornfields tasseled out, past
vine-wrapped barns, square bales of scrap metal
heaped beside the tracks outside of Ashland,

past two women visiting on a narrow plant-filled
porch, past the aquamarine geometries of backyard pools,
past herds of cattle, heads down, shadows humped,
indefinite, wrenching up the generosities of grass
far, far yet from the city once innocent of its riches,
its towering heights, which now knows, like its poor sisters
all across the earth, the fist out of the sky, the shock,
the fire, the smoke-choked darkness, and descent.

Hunting for a Christmas Tree after Dark

A sudden mildness in the cold field.
Scraps of snow still strewn on the hillside.
The net of stars cast out overhead.
The shapes of old cedars come toward me
familiar as loved bodies approaching
from a long way off.
The creek in a hurry, as full of itself
as a zipper, the slow-melting snow.

I can hardly make out the rock fence
wavering up the hill, cold stone
on cold stone, stacked together
by unknown hands so many years ago.

How grateful I am for this moment of peace
my body has made with gravity, this
pulling things out of their places
and holding them in,
like Orion the hunter, who, when I blink,
seems to throw his leg over the low fence
of the horizon and climb into this bound with me.

Up ahead, looking for the one perfect tree,
my cousin John. His lantern bobs through
the dark meadow. He raises the globe
of light over and over in prospect.
I hang back, feeling rich in the black
waste, safe in this bowl of earth,
with rocks outcropping in the flattened grass,

trees wet, dirt sweetened by the downhill run-off
of all fear. Though the Interstate throbs
and the town lights bleed into the blot
of circling trees, from here the stars redeem
the dark that makes them shine.

Penelope's Night Out

Last night the fall crescent drifted down a summer sky.
The crickets sang their eternal one-note chorus.
You and I went to a party in a lovely room filled
with likenesses of the hosts in the beauty
of their youth, and with the books they cherish.
The room opened to a porch that gave upon a woods.
I watched its stand of handsome tree trunks fade
in the twilight. I chatted up a temptress in whose thrall
you once were held. After we drained the sweet liquor
from the last cubes in our glasses, we said good-bye
to friends, and to the pleasant new acquaintances.

We stepped into a moonless darkness and drove,
companionably touching hands, thighs in the golden light
of the dashboard. At home, we stepped out of our clothes
and laughed again at a conversation I had overheard.
We spoke, too, of Calypso's presence there. Then
as we lay beside each other, sleepily touching, with our
mouths, our fingers, our viscous skin, a wakefulness
surprised us like a wave, rolled us into the ecstasy
of this unlikely night, and dropped us, sleeping
soundly as you did, Odysseus, surrounded by all
your treasure, on the strange shore of home.

Their Bed

Tonight I go to sleep to thunder over the fields
and summer rainfall like my mother's voice
when she lay beside my father in their bed,
each of its posts heavy as a tree.
Rain dripped through trumpet vines
outside their open window.
I knew they pleased each other: he loved
her milky body, her hair like fire,
her fingers always doing. She loved
his wide laugh, his ease with cattle,
his biceps, hard as hedge balls,
that he squeezed in knots for us to feel.
In their bed they lay notched like forks
in the kitchen drawer. From my bed I heard
them talk about the rain—it brings on hay,
makes big tobacco leaves. Stiff with listening,
I hear what they heard (the fall of water,
heaving trees), and I drift away, carried
into the dark on swift currents of their comfort.

In the Moment of My Death:
For My Father

You were simple, I suppose,
delighted by life
so that sickness and death
came to you as a surprise
out of the shadows of your heart.

In the moment of my death
may your old happiness light my way,
and the image of your face
smiling, happy at my coming,
be a lantern in the dark.

An English professor at the University of Kentucky, Jane Gentry Vance (published as **Jane Gentry**) was born in Lexington and raised in nearby Athens. The people and landscape of Athens, with its tobacco and cattle farms, molded her, she says, "into whatever it is I am. Its shape is the shape of my writing."

Gentry is a recent Kentucky poet laureate (2007–2008), and has published two collections of poetry—*Portrait of the Artist as a White Pig* and *A Garden in Kentucky.* Her poems have appeared widely in journals, including the *Sewanee Review, Hollins Critic, Harvard Magazine,* and *New Virginia Review,* and in numerous anthologies, among them *Hero's Way: Contemporary Poems in the Mythic Tradition* (Prentice-Hall), *Cries of the Spirit: A Celebration of Women's Spirituality* (Beacon Press), *The American Voice Anthology of Poetry* and *The Kentucky Anthology* (University Press of Kentucky). She has also been awarded two Al Smith Fellowships from the Kentucky Arts Council and has held fellowships at Yaddo in Saratoga Springs, New York, and at the Virginia Center for the Creative Arts in Lynchburg.

Gentry lists a stellar lineup of literary influences: Shakespeare, Emily Dickinson, W. B. Yeats, Robert Frost, T. S. Eliot, Randall Jarrell, Elizabeth Bishop, James Dickey, Denise Levertov, Howard Nemerov (who was her teacher), Sylvia Plath, Maxine Kumin, and Anne Sexton.

On "Hunting for a Christmas Tree after Dark," Gentry writes that "this poem was occasioned by my annual quest for a just-right cedar tree, a hunt that has gone on in my family along Boone's Creek since my grandfather, born in 1860, was a child. This particular search I undertook with my cousin, John Dulin. He collects lanterns, so that's what he took to light our way as we began looking for the Christmas tree in the near-dark fields. It was important to me to write this poem because the unusual conditions of this search somehow connected it to the many earlier ones, and connected me to a strange home countryside where time, darkness and light, life and death seemed for a moment to be all the same thing, all of a piece, and full of peace."

RICHARD
Taylor

b. 1941

On Whapping My Index Finger
with a Roofing Hammer

This time it happens on the garage
nailing shingles, driving
steel on steel through asphalt, felt,
and poplar sheathing tacked down
before McKinley was shot.

Spring is still a murmur,
the yard simmering with patches
of scrawny green, wands
in the water maples
blushing lavender
against the sober ridge.

From his pickup window
Jim Haney waves, yells up
to ask if I'm doing any good—
just enough distraction
to skew the dropping hammer,
his wife and teenage daughter
wincing in the cab
when I shout the most basic verb
that pain can summon.

Yowling, offending the righteous—
imprecision has other costs.
Add the cuticle's shattered moon,
the blue-back scarab

already trapped beneath the nail.
This throbbing cannot match
even one forsythia
whose swollen buds muscle just now
their yellow liberation into bloom.

Imagining My Own Death

I can envision many deaths—
stumbling into the cistern
on a July evening after too much
chilled Zinfandel, crickets clicking
their symphonies in the grass.
This is only one of them.

Or, instead of Pliny the Elder
sniffing a fatal whiff
of smoking casserole under Vesuvius,
standing in my own backyard
under the white throat
of a colossal sycamore that snaps
while I ponder the genealogy
of snow or a word to describe
the sounds of falling water.

But the worst is sitting
in a meeting of the sub committee
for administrative review
convened to measure the efficiency
of systems and processes,
the sands of the hourglass
sifting into a Mojave
of lost time, irrecoverable moments,
the turning of thousands
of tiny wheels that produce
motion but no movement.

Water Hauling on Sunday Morning

Pulling onto Coffeetree Drive
near the pumping station
to draw my weekly load,
I scan for residential deer,
spotting three in scruffy woods
a stone's throw off the hardtop.

Tame, safe on posted ground,
two do not bother
to lift their stretched necks.
Only one, an edgy doe, swivels
her tapered head and stares,
eyeing my credentials.

Calmed, she turns back toward
the browsers on legs as tense,
as frail, as wickets.
I speak no language to tell her
open season starts Saturday, no
code to tap out muffled thunder
that will thrum the hills.

Instead, as the craned pipe spews
white pillars downward in the tank,
I watch the water rise
and hear myself intone
above the shushing swirl
inside the void,
"Lie low next week, stay close."
This Sunday ritual is my church,
these deer my stony habitat of hope.

The Lava Beds at Pompeii

Using a steel rod, Guiseppe Fiorelli
first tapped the crust in 1863,
finding hollows where humans
had dried up and all but vanished.
In these pockets he poked holes,
filling the curious voids with plaster.

When it set, he pried out
a plaster man, suffocating,
clawing at his underclothes,
then another clutching some coins.
Next, a woman hugging a child,
two gladiators doomed in their cells
still manacled to the wall,
even a dog straining at its leash.

What they hold in common
is August 24, 79 A.D., a day
when morning went night
and rained pumice, rivers
of volcanic ash flowing down
the Via dell' Abbondanze
to smother it under twenty feet
of sulphuric silt.

Street by street, yard by yard,
Fiorelli reclaimed what he could:
black loaves from the baker's oven,
a cup unfinished on the potter's wheel,
a table set for noon.

Now, after two millennia,
the victims plead through museum glass
still writhe against extinction,
affirming all that is human
in the tension of an upraised hand,
a gaping mouth—
agonies more eloquent than speech.

An Inner Tour of Shaker Village at Pleasant Hill, Kentucky

In the Center Family dwelling
where the brethren and sisters
ascend to dream on separate stairs,
I feel an invisible razory line
that splits the sexes.
It hovers among the dust motes
that drift toward immaculate floors.
It populates the air, weighs
down the segregated tables
off which the Shakers consumed
their bounty in communal silence—
only a snicking of tableware
unsettling their pious concentration.

Even from the peep holes
where the elders scrutinized
the sabbath dancers,
who stamped and wriggled
with the zeal of martyrs
as they shook off Satan,
there must have been carnal lapses—
infractions of the lingering eye,
lust among the cabbages,
or glimmerings over aqua jars
filled with the jellied plum
and fallen peach, or furtive touchings
as flax seeds were packeted
to green the Lower South.

Though records show Mahalia Polly,
frustrated in marriage five times,
finally eloped with a village miller,
the evidence admits few "private unions."
Instead, the Believers must have thrived
on remembered warmth, the heat
preserved in stone walls after sundown.

Into each room sunlight shines—
the same splendor that kissed
the gritty road down which lay
what they described ingenuously
as "the world." Inside each room
there is an anteroom, a closet
with an inner window
lit so long as there are beams
of outside radiance, but dimmer,
fainter, still sufficient—what
students of design now refer to,
with praise, as "borrowed light."

Notes for a Manual on Form

for C. G.

Asked for an infallible guide,
an unerring rule to prescribe
how one word mates another
in perfect union, how another

offends proportion or causes
sonal imbalance, or how one
takes its place among others
to bond with proper tension,

a measure of grace, a promise
of durability—I answer with
the only insight I know, from
a nameless black mason whose

gnarled hands, palms worn
to the pink, could size a rock
and slap up each day 16 feet
of fence that was "horse high,

bull strong, and pig tight,"
when others at best cobbled
half as much with a tenth
the starch, a quarter the heft.

Asked how he could do it,
how summon the right rock
to fill just the right chink,
he said, "I gots the stone eye."

Richard Taylor is a professor of English at Kentucky State University, where he has taught literature and creative writing since 1975. Raised in Louisville, he holds a Ph.D. in English from the University of Kentucky.

Taylor, a sixth-generation Kentuckian who served as Kentucky poet laureate from 1999 to 2001, is the author of six collections of poetry, two historical novels, and several works of nonfiction and history. His most recent book is *Sue Mundy: A Novel of the Civil War.*

Among his many awards and honors are an Al Smith Creative Writing Fellowship from the Kentucky Arts Council, the Distinguished Professor Award from Kentucky State University in 1992, a Fulbright lectureship, and two NEA Creative Writing Fellowships.

Taylor's earliest literary influence was his uncle, Louis Dey, who, Taylor says, taught him a love of language and challenged him to look up any word he didn't know. His uncle also gave him a subscription to the Landmark book series on American history, from which Taylor dates his lifelong interest in history, especially Kentucky history. "And I wrote poems in high school," he recalls, "which my teachers charitably did not much discourage."

Before settling into the life of a writer and English professor, Taylor got a law degree at the University of Kentucky, then worked in a judicial system program in which prisoners convicted of misdemeanors not involving violence were released on their own recognizance. Taylor practiced law for fewer than four months, getting out, as he likes to say, in the public interest.

Of "On Whapping My Index Finger with a Roofing Hammer," Taylor says: "In this poem, I tried to get at the experience of pain and the loss of control that it occasions, as well as its comic possibilities. The 'me' in this poem is a character very much like myself, a klutz who receives the brunt of his misdoings. I like to write poems that face reality with a sense of openness, a willingness to acknowledge our humanness, especially our shortcomings in which others can recognize and affirm their own. Once I saw the similarity between extremes—the throbbing in the swollen finger, the pulse of spring itself and the garish yellow of the forsythia—tying the roofing poem to spring was an easy choice. It is these little rhymes of experience that interest me, that can make a poem."

JOE
Survant

b. 1942

Anne Waters

December 28, 1842

She is gone.
A door in the earth
opened. She
fell through
our lives and
entered it. I
would have followed
but Alph and Mama
stopped me. The
door closed heavy
above her and I
could not go.
Now nature stands
between us, the
dark cedars an
admonition, and a
wall. For three days
I've sought that door,
felt along the smooth
earth for
fast-fading edges,
Alph and God
standing in my way.
Then I find it.
I cross the meadow
in the worn track
of cattle where
it lies gleaming
dully in the winter

light. The cold makes
my feet ache, but I give
myself to it, sinking slowly
into silence and
what I hope is light.

Anne Waters

December 21, 1862

Dreamed I had my baby
back,
held her in a blanket
before the fire
and rubbed her
arms and legs
until she moved again,
and then began to cry.
I was suddenly
filled up,
like something solid
had entered my body,
or an arm lost long ago
had returned
to swell the empty sleeve and
drive away the phantom pain.
We rocked and rocked
before that fire
which blazed impossibly,
devouring the cold
and pushing back the dark
around the house.
I ran to tell the news,
but when I lifted
the cover there was
only the piglet I'd
tried to save last spring,
already cold and still.
Then I was myself again.

What was here
was still around me,
what was gone
was absent as before.
Outside a cold rain
fell blankly on the roof
and in the empty fields.

Alpheus Waters

February 20, 1863

Gone!
While we were
in Owensville,
Isaac and Sarah
Dolly and Robert,
and with them
the wagon and half
the smokehouse stores.
Well, let them have it.
We shared the bloody
work between us.

I should not blame
their going,
yet I do,
the deception of it.
Somewhere words failed,
more likely were not spoken.
The unsaid
like fine cracks
spreading through ice
under great strain.

I do not know
how such solitude
will sit,
Anne silent
in her kitchen
while I work

alone in the barn.
Yet they must go
their way,
black from white,
resolving the gray.

Such stillness now.
Anne fixes supper
while I milk the cow.
The warm beast-smell
fills the stable's air.
In the dusk
I lean my head
against Bessie's side.
She stands compliant
while I work,
quiet in the
stolid way of cows.

Alpheus Waters

July 13, 1882

Suckering is almost
beyond me now.
Working each plant from
top to bottom for the
small gummy shoots
one for every leaf
in the hot August sun
is some of the hardest
work I've ever done.
My chest fills with the
stooping heat, the air
beneath the leaves moves
only with my motion.
I cannot see Tom or his
son Abe where they work.
Each of us moves in a
little space bounded narrowly
by tall plants and broad leaves.
Even the shade is hot.

Heat thickens around me,
minutes come faster
bumping into one another
in their hurry to be done.
The tobacco stands over me
breathing as I breathe,
its exhaling full of sweet narcotic.
My lungs and skin burn with it.
The air shimmering with heat and

light
lifts me out of myself.
I try to stand and call to Tom
but the dirt between the rows
quickens with the revolving earth.
My chest explodes.

Anne Waters

September 7, 1882

This fall comes early
and hard.
Ears of uncut corn
drop in the dry fields
and tobacco withers
silently in the barn.
Already
in the heart
of the hackberry tree
five chosen leaves
turn red as blood
and the light takes
on a fearful intensity.
In the evening
I walk through the
fields down to where
the river goes
into the ground.
Once I heard her voice
in the falling water.
I don't believe it
will be silent now.
He is wherever I look,
in the horse lot,
in the barn,
and on my eyes
like a light-fed image
that will not fade.
What does nature know

of those who've entered her,
or of us who still work
and walk about the world?
Perhaps those who die
do not drop out of the world.
They remain.
The world takes them,
and they are changed.

At the Camp Meeting

I. Susan Rose

I knew he'd come
so I put on my yellow
dress and combed
rosewater through my hair.
I studied him secretly,
learning his lean strong limbs
as he moved among the crowd.
When I saw him take
a piece of the buttermilk
pie I'd baked,
I looked straight at him
and he at me. My
face felt warm, but

I didn't look away.
Brother David began
to speak and everyone
moved up around him,
but I hung back and
stepped into the woods
and followed a little trail
hardly worn at all
until I came to an
open place where the tall
trees held off the brush
and made a little cove.
Bill entered through
the trees and all
the birds were hushed.

He just came up
and kissed me
where I stood.
Little cared I for
camp meetings then,
and I raised my arms
to hold him
and kissed him back.
Behind us the singing
had begun, sending
out the old question
among the oak and swaying gum,
"Shall we gather at the river?"
And we did.

II. Bill Balcom

When I took
a piece of Susie's
buttermilk pie,
I saw her looking,
and when I ate
I imagined
her taste.

I looked and ate,
humming with hunger.
The meeting flowed
around us, but
she didn't look away,
then drifted out
on the crowd's edge.

I watched her
yellow dress
disappear in the woods
like the raised flag
of a fleeing deer,
then circled around
before her.

We met
in a little clearing.
Neither of us spoke,
just came together.
I kissed her there and
she kissed me, then
undid her long black hair.

Kentucky's poet laureate from 2003 to 2004, **Joe Survant** is the author of four collections of poetry—*Anne & Alpheus, 1842–1882,* winner of the Arkansas Poetry Prize, *The Presence of Snow in the Tropics, We Will All Be Changed,* which won the State Street Press Award, and *Rafting Rise,* a collection of narrative poems set in the Green River Basin near Owensboro just before the United States' entry into World War I. His other awards include an Al Smith Fellowship in Poetry, the Frankfort Arts Chapbook Award, a Fulbright Fellowship to Malaysia, and a fellowship from the National Endowment for the Humanities.

Survants's poems have appeared in many literary magazines, including *Prairie Schooner, Chelsea, Stand Magazine,* and the *American Voice.* His work has also been included in a dozen anthologies, most recently *The Kentucky Anthology: Two Hundred Years of Writing in the Bluegrass.*

A professor emeritus of Western Kentucky University's English department, Survant is a native of Owensboro, Kentucky, on the Ohio River, a circumstance that he counts as one of the main influences on his writing and on his decision to become a poet. He underscores that water—ponds, streams, and rivers, both surface and below ground—is a constant presence in his poetry. He attended the University of Kentucky and then the University of Delaware, where he earned a Ph.D. in English. Before beginning a teaching career that spanned four decades, he worked in construction and on a factory machine that "extruded rubber hoses."

Survant says he was moved to write for the first time at age eleven when he read Clifford D. Simak's far-future novel *City.* At thirteen he was jolted to attempt poetry when he read Rimbaud's *A Season in Hell* and Kipling's narrative verse, where he discovered the compelling contraries of narrative and lyric language at the edge of meaning. Other influences he cites are William Wordsworth, John Keats, Robert Creeley, Gary Snyder, and Robert Bly.

On "Anne Waters, December 21, 1862": "Nearing the twentieth anniversary of her daughter's death in 1842, Anne has an archetypal dream. She dreams that she has her dead child back only to have the dream shift into nightmare and to awaken to find that 'what was gone / was absent as before.' The death of Catherine is the defining tragedy of Anne's life and of her forty-year marriage to Alpheus. The dream is a fulcrum in the middle of her marriage, in her middle age, and in the middle of the chaos of the Civil War. She awakens to the world as it is, a barrier she can't see beyond. This image runs throughout the book, below the surface of the narrative, like an underground stream."

JONATHAN
Greene

b. 1943

The Ideal Reader

Some use for old poems—

the mice in the basement
found them, chewed over
what the critics ignored,
a letter-by-letter
close reading!

An audience the mailing lists
overlooked, my work judged good
enough to live in, Grade A
nesting matter!

Mao

The West can't
understand it.

Five hundred million
wait upon his words

more than on
the weather

but instead of
some small worry

of government
he is trying

to get right
a poem on

The Great March
or the feeling

of Autumn
in his life.

Scarecrow Poems

1.
The scarecrow,
stuffed full of straw,
looks better fed than
the farmer!

2.
A gift tuxedo
found in the junk store.
Thanks, but of no use to me. . . .

But what a
fancy scarecrow
I now have!

Recollections of Bass Rhythms of Hip-Hop Heard from a Distant Van

Right about the time
bats in the eaves
bed down for day,
the birds at dawn
start to carry on

while soon

drivers deaf
to the green world
try with their woofers
to dominate the pulse
of the world.

Waiting

Works sculpted in marble,
blown in glass,

shaped in bowls
by master potters—

that, after years of use,
the simplest action,

the same as a hundred times before,
can suddenly shatter—

hidden fault lines
in the heart of things.

Jonathan Greene was born and grew up in New York City and moved to San Francisco in the early 1960s, where he founded Gnomon Press. A Kentucky resident since 1966, he has published more than sixty books with the Gnomon Press imprint, including works by Robert Duncan, Wendell Berry, Cid Corman, James Still, Jim Wayne Miller, and Gurney Norman.

He is the author of twenty-eight books and chapbooks, most recently *Fault Lines, Hut Poems, Heart Matters,* and *The Death of a Kentucky Coffee-Tree & Other Poems.* His poems have appeared in *Origin, Poetry,* the *American Voice,* the *Quarterly Review of Literature,* and several anthologies. Greene has also received fellowships from the National Endowment for the Arts, the Southern Federation of State Arts Agencies, and the Kentucky Arts Council.

He has given readings at colleges across the country, including Cornell University, Indiana University, Bennington College, the Poetry Center at San Francisco State, and the University of Kentucky. He cites as his earliest literary influences William Carlos Williams, Gary Snyder, Charles Olson, and two teachers—Ralph Ellison and Robert Lowell.

Greene lives on a farm near Frankfort with his wife, Dobree Adams, a weaver and photographer. They raise horses, llamas, donkeys, and chickens, "among other creatures," Greene says. He also continues to do freelance book design and has won a number of awards in this field.

On "Mao": "I use the figure of Mao as a poet-ruler, even though one Chinese scholar friend says all or most of the poems attributed to Mao were actually written by a ghost writer! And I know that Mao was a despot and that his failed Great Leap Forward caused millions of deaths, and then his anti-intellectual Cultural Revolution destroyed much of the cultural heritage of his own country and resulted in more deaths. In a later poem, 'Dynasty 101,' I am more realistic about this part of Chinese history."

VIVIAN
Shipley

b. 1943

With My Father outside the
West Wing of Hospice

The silence between us has softened
like the fishing rag you gave me to keep

my fingers from getting finned while
I cleaned bluegills. A squirrel is inching

up the pole of the bird feeder we watch.
It's a rewind of Buster Keaton playing hero

in *The Three Ages*, catching a drainpipe
that swings him around a hundred

and eighty degrees to a pole he slides
down. You can't smile. I think Kentucky,

October squirrels under a black walnut
that will mark your feet when I bury

you in Howe Valley. A rebel like you,
not to be outdone, our Yankee squirrel

grabs the feeder's dish and flips,
a trapeze artist doing a double whammy.

You whisper, see what can come
of holding on, what not giving up can do.

Just when I thought I had stopped
my heart, you start it beating again.

First Ice

Unlike my sorrow, which has started to scab,
grass has not closed over this raw red
Kentucky clay. Over eight months now.
My father's plot is still unmarked, a rupture

in my heart that needs to find a name
to heal. I've come back to these hills to see
the communion altar the Ladies' Guild
built in Howe Valley Methodist Church

with my donation, to measure other stones
so Daddy's will not be the tallest. He avoided
standing out, showing off in life, and there
is no reason I can think of he should in death.

Marble I had chosen yesterday is too black,
too glossy; I'll have to go back in the morning
to Cheneyville, prove Mr. Crum was right,
that it's women who always change their minds.

What I want is a pint bottle of Wild Turkey,
a jelly glass, to sit in my cousin Sue's kitchen
and nip at Jim's country ham. Instead, to thank
Hansel Pile for putting a wreath on my father's

grave, I head out across Hardin County, a place
so religious even grapevines are tied to crosses.
Sure enough, I find pictures of Jesus, head
wrapped in thorns, cracked linoleum floors,

deviled eggs sprinkled with paprika. Minding
my manners, I admire trophies won by Hansel's
bulls, linger over the photograph of Sammy,
his grand champion at the Indiana Fair. Done

with the judge's ring, Hansel tells me his secret:
a donkey to lead cattle around, get them used
to a rope. No blue ribbons for the donkey.
All night every night, it walked and walked,

stupid, helpless, tethered as it was to one halter,
then another. In winter, Hansel turned the donkey
out to pasture without food. I imagine its cracked
hooves, scraping at what was in frozen ground,

stumbling through February, monotony broken
by breath, a shadow moving from tuft to tuft.
The donkey knew its duty here, knew its worth,
knew its only chance for hay, corn. A small gray

memory, each spring it came back to the pen
as I do to Howe Valley, these hills, to my father.
Braided to reason, to its life, I think of the donkey,
of what we accept if we wear it long enough

like the rope hooked to the bull, like octagonal links
of a gold necklace I finger, like the weight of grief.

Corner of Bellefonte and Heather Way,
Lexington, Kentucky

My first Father's Day without a father, I avoid
Walgreen's rack of cards. Thirty years of a tightrope
shuffle between Kentucky hills and Connecticut shore,

dirt roads to interstate, I have come back to buy
a marker for his grave. Naming and dating my father
will not hold his life, but what is remembered

in stone will not be lost. I don't long to bring him
back to where he was, blue velour chair with a motor
to lift him away from pain. Last summer, I emptied

my parents' home of all that would never need to be
disposed of again. I would not haggle over what
had no price: Daddy's tools, benches he had built

to hold them. Fooling neighbors who circled, wolves
one day, coyotes the next, who figured on the last day,
I'd have to give his workshop away, I moved the router,

drill press, radial-arm saw, lathe, jointer, the days,
the years my father had spent with them. I even shipped
ten foot boards of walnut and oak Daddy had hauled

out of Hardin County. Turning the corner of Bellefonte,
I wasn't surprised. I had predicted what would become
of their house with the new owners. Knowing what

cannot be eased in the heart, that what I want is a father,
a parachute that will let me fall and fall again, I will
not ask to go inside. Lawn barer than my oriental rug,

there used to be zinnias for cutting, and Daddy always
mowed the grass on the diagonal. Windows wide open,
the garage door is not shut. Past bloom, iris are not

sheared to fans; the front walk has never been edged.
Once solid as a Magritte, boxwood ringing the yard
has holes big enough to dart through. Keeping the hedge

topped, my father fortressed my childhood. He is dead;
no one shears it to shoulder height. No corners with
shadows coupling, where can I curl into a ball and hide?

Coma: Bachus Hospital, Norwich, Connecticut

I key in *CONNELLAN* on a robot's pad that leads me
to your room in intensive care. You are stiller, older,
and quiet—a phone is not squeezed into your shoulder.

Your daughter puts a hearing aid in your good ear
in spite of the face a nurse makes. My hands rusty,
I pray for words to wing into gulls so you, Poet Laureate

of Connecticut, can laugh with me about the bag of urine
with the brand name *BARD* hooked on your bed.
A doctor says touch and hearing are the last senses to go;

I tunnel a finger, my love, into your hand. Did the stroke
erase running out of gas after our reading at Stone Soup,
hiking Massachusetts Turnpike until the church-going

Baptist took us to the toll station? You thanked him with
a Dixie cup of Wild Turkey. A thief, the clot has bagged
that memory and others: the waiter uncorking champagne

at the Pierre Hotel before your Shelley Memorial Prize,
smoke from fringe of blue jeans Bill Packard set on fire.
The off-season rate in Maine motels with room service

was the makeshift paradise you gave to your wife. If love
of this earth is a way to enter heaven, you will be there,
trying to tear a hole back into this world for fried oysters,

onion rings, lobster dripping in butter. The grandson
of an Irish immigrant who fled to Rockland, Maine, you
were seven when your mother died. Saying she'd gone

to care for another boy who needed her more, your father
took you and your brother to her grave each year, thinking
you'd figure it out. Death will end your childhood dream,

your mother never in it. She will be at the kitchen door
waiting, hands holding muffins studded in blueberries
with names like *rabbiteyes* and *Tifblue*. Leo, go to her now.

A professor of English at Connecticut State University and editor of *Connecticut Review*, **Vivian Shipley** was born and raised in the small northern Kentucky town of Elsmere. Her family on both sides were farmers, and Shipley remembers spending "happy time" every summer on her grandparents' farms. After earning a B.A. and an M.A. in English from the University of Kentucky, Shipley got married and moved to New Haven, Connecticut, where she has lived ever since.

Shipley's twelve books and chapbooks of poetry include *Hardboot: Poems, New & Old; Gleanings: Old Poems, New Poems; Fair Haven;* and *Devil's Lane.* Her poems have appeared in the *American Scholar, Shenandoah,* the *Southern Review,* the *Iowa Review,* and the *Mississippi Review,* and in dozens of anthologies, including *Southern Appalachian Poetry, The Anthology of New England Writers,* and *The Kentucky Anthology.*

Shipley's many awards for poetry include the Paterson Award for Sustained Literary Achievement, the *River Styx* International Poetry Prize, and the Hart Crane Poetry Prize. She says her poetry has been heavily influenced by Robert Frost, T. S. Eliot, and Wallace Stevens, and by contemporary poets Maxine Kumin, Sharon Olds, and Ted Kooser.

When, at age thirty-two, she began writing poems, she recalls that she first turned back to her Kentucky roots to "try to preserve my rural heritage and celebrate the honesty and decency of my relatives that still sustain me. I often return to Kentucky in my poems to record family stories."

On "First Ice": "This poem is a literal description of my experience picking out a gravestone for my father's grave. When I went to visit Hansel Pile and heard the story of the donkey that led bulls around the ring to train them, I knew I would write a poem about him in order to preserve his memory. For me, the story also became a metaphor for how I was beginning to heal after my father's death. The challenge that I faced in writing the poem was in controlling the emotion—not letting the poem become sentimental. It was very reassuring to me when Baron Wormser, a poet I respect a great deal, picked this poem as the 2001 winner of the Robert Frost Foundation Prize."

PHILIP
St. Clair

b. 1944

Menace from Space

When the creatures from Mars came down in the Fifties
Grownups were really naive—they thought everyone knew
What a white flag was, what the word *friend* meant,
That a man in a black coat with a certain kind of collar
Spoke with God's mouth, and shouldn't be killed.

He was the first to go, striding toward that red-hot crater
With a Bible held over his head like a grenade,
Saying *The Lord is My Shepherd*, singing *Lead, Kindly Light*,
Then getting hit right in the gut with a cosmic heat-ray—
Nothing left but ashes where his shadow used to be.

Then the college kid, who said *jeepers* a lot, blazed away
From the hip with his old man's twelve-gauge pump,
But they torched him too. The Mexican got away, damn near
Stripping every gear in his beat-up pickup truck
To warn the small town, where the young atomic scientist

Was at a hoedown, dancing with the preacher's daughter—
Tight sweaters all through the movie. Then the lights went out,
Came back on, and everyone's watch had stopped: bobby pins
Clung to them like icicles on hubcaps. *Magnetized!*
The scientist said. *By an energy source unknown on earth!*

It got better when the Martians built their fighters,
But they looked too much like manta rays. They could melt tanks
As if they were made from plastic, turn our biggest bombers
To puffs of greasy smoke, but the dumb-ass general
Kept on sending our soldiers to get burned up for fishfood.

Drop the fucking H-bomb! we shouted, bouncing Milk-Duds
Right off his nose to get his attention. It worked:
He looked us in the eye, said *No—weapons of such destructive power*
Are too great a hazard for our civilians. Bullshit! we shouted,
And razzed him with kazoos made from Jujube boxes.

But soon they had to try that too, after the preacher's daughter
Almost got felt up by a three-fingered monster
And the Capitol Building was a pile of busted marble,
But after the flash and the tall mushroom cloud
They were still in the air, didn't even seem pissed.

The whole thing ended in church: everyone was praying
By a stained-glass window that hadn't been smashed yet,
And the preacher's daughter and the atomic scientist
Fell in love, hugged and smooched, which made us
Pop Coke cups, blow farts on the backs of our hands.

All of a sudden, all over the world, their ships
Wobbled and whined, stalled out, crashed—everyone cheered!
Then a door opened, and a slimy, sucker-fingered hand
Slowly eased out, twitched once, was still: *Bacteria!*
The scientist said. *All of them killed by the Common Cold!*

Wow! we shouted as choirs, harps, and scripture verses
Thundered out of the screen, and in the front row one of us,
Transported by God's mercy and the power of tiny microbes,
Threw half a box of popcorn in the air—the bloom of victory,
Frozen in the hard, white light of the projection booth.

Last Night

I dreamed I was talking,
And when I agreed with what I said

I shouted *That's right!*
And I woke myself up. Now I wish

It hadn't happened—
That dream was a good dream,

And even though I can't remember
Where I was, who was with me,

I wanted to go back.
I wish I hadn't been

So eager to push myself on
Whoever I was there. Down here

I'm politeness incarnate—
Modest, non-violent, easy-going—

But sometimes in dreams
I pick fights, sass, act like a jerk

In general: this never happens
When I'm awake. What is it

Inside me that makes me
Argue with bikers, smack angels

On the back of the head,
Anger pretty women who want to

Know me better, get thrown out
Of the best clubs in Heaven?

Society

My brother cannot see us when we visit: his eyes
Are glazed and dead, and the half-shut lids
Do not flutter to keep them wet. Yesterday
We carried all his magazines downstairs:
Town & Country, Vanity Fair, European Life.
The nurse has told us what to expect
When the myriad sieves within him
Begin to clog and close: *hallucinate*, she said,
A gentle word that rustles and taps
Like a drift of mapleseeds, a clinical word
As bright and naked as reason itself,
And those of the invisible who may be
Hovering above his bed are of no importance
To our busy, seasoned caregiver
When she climbs the stairs to his room.

Now we are only voices and hands
Who disturb the stale air that clings to him
As we stroke his head and whisper and clean,
As he says *My God who are all these people
Is this heaven it must be heaven*
And as his shoulders tense in the effort
Of reaching out, he turns his face
Up to the corner of his room,
Brings one thin hand to an open mouth
In the ancient gesture of astonishment,
Tries to wave at the people who wait
Past the black, empty trees and the powerlines
Heavy with dulling ice, past the twin chimneys
On the steel mill behind our fence:
So glad you could come   How marvelous

Into the Wires

Home again after my brother's funeral,
And when I go to bed the radio will not work:
I flick the chromed selector switch
Through both its possibilities, and all I hear
Is a quick, faint rustle in the woofers
As if the music has been snatched away.
Then the coils on top of the stove refuse to heat:
I pull the plug, unscrew a dust-flocked plate,
Pry out both fuses in their thin glass reliquaries
And find them uncorrupted, like Ramses or King Tut.
My sister calls with news: light bulbs have popped
All through a cousin's house in Houston,
And in L.A. a tongue of acrid, brassy smoke
Snaked out of my uncle's brand-new TV set
Right in the middle of primetime.
Maybe he's letting us know he's back, she says.

If he's done all this, what does it mean?
Is this his lesson that an afterlife exists,
Or is he a Victorian trope brought up to date:
Doomed, in another place and time, to rattle chains
In scullery or billiardroom, but now transformed
To a Nineties apparition who's a jetstream of electrons
In spite of himself, endowed with subatomic power
To the limits of thought and light, able to melt down
All the slender circuits in our hardware,
Sidle up to us through the cables to our houses
Past microchip and motherboard, free to scramble
Our high-resolution, state-of-the-art reception

To let us know he's out there somewhere, perhaps
Watching from the inside of our picture tubes,
Waiting until we've drowsed off on the couch
To shout through speakers, shock us awake.

Philip St. Clair is a professor of humanities at Ashland Community and Technical College in Ashland, Kentucky, where he has taught since 1991. He has published four books of poetry: *In the Thirty-Nine Steps*, *At the Tent of Heaven*, *Little-Dog-of-Iron*, and *Acid Creek*. His poems have appeared in many journals and magazines, including the *Beloit Poetry Journal*, the *Gettysburg Review*, *Harper's*, *Poetry Review* (London), and *Shenandoah*. St. Clair's awards include grants from the National Endowment for the Arts and the Kentucky Arts Council; he won the Helen Bullis Prize from *Poetry Northwest* in 1986.

Born in Warren, Ohio, St. Clair spent four years in the U.S. Air Force during the Vietnam War, then earned a B.A. and M.A. in English and an M.L.S. degree in library science from Kent State University. His interest in poetry then led him to an M.F.A. degree in creative writing from Bowling Green State University in Ohio.

St. Clair says his most important literary influence was the Beat poets. "I was astonished at what they were able to do with language, and I very much admired their irreverence toward much of what went on in Eisenhower's America. I also realized that beneath that irreverence was a protest against the status quo and a strong desire for social and political justice."

A later important poetic influence, he says, was Jim Wayne Miller, one of Kentucky's strongest literary voices, who died in 1996. In the fall of 1994, a few years after St. Clair came to Eastern Kentucky to teach, he attended the annual writers' conference in Hindman, Kentucky, where he heard Miller lecture on Appalachian literature. "This sparked additional interest in writing, and soon after I moved from Ashland to Rush—in the Appalachian mountains of Carter County, Kentucky—in 1996, I began to think about writing poetry that centered around the Appalachian portion of Route 60, four miles from where I live."

St. Clair advises beginning writers of poetry to read all they can, including poetry written in languages other than English, to "know thy predecessors and respect them," and to think of the act of writing as an occasion for discovery and joy.

On "Society": "My older brother, David, was a writer of fiction and nonfiction and, as a correspondent for *Time* magazine, had traveled all over the world. In 1990 he came back to his mother's small house in Warren, Ohio, with advanced colon cancer. My sisters and I helped care for him during his final days and were thus witnesses to the great mystery of a human being passing from one existence into another. I hope the poem captures his astonishment—and ours."

JEFF Worley

b. 1947

Sleeping with Two Women

As I remember it, we emptied
three bottles of Mateus
and wedged ourselves

onto their third-story windowsill.
We watched the snow pile up
around us, one fat rectangular flake

after another shuffling down
to erase every step we'd taken,
my '59 Chevy disappearing

under a helmet of snow.
We had time for such deliberate
watching then, Wichita, 1973.

And I remember us laughing
about Sharon's ex—a guy
who kept tires in their bedroom—

and Barbara's story of the time
she slept with her brother
on a family vacation in Minnesota:

Here, feel this, he said, Barbara
screaming at her first encounter
with a boner, but laughing now.

The snow kept tumbling down,
and I don't know who suggested it,
but I remember the slow undressing

as if we were figures being carved
in ivory. The candle in the bedroom
strobed light onto the lip of the bottle

I was holding like a trophy. And when
Barbara's panties finally fell away
like a white petal, we all piled into bed

laughing at our nakedness—
no rippling muscles, not a sculpted
buttock among us. I nudged in

between them, and what happened
in that bed, under the Niagara of snow,
candlelight drawing hieroglyphs

on the walls, was simply that they inched
toward me, close enough so that
we were touching and not touching.

Perhaps passion flared up in some other
candlelit room that night. Here,
I reached out my hands and felt them

settle, lightly (forty heartbeats or so
away from sleep), on those warm separate
continents. Perfectly at home, perfectly lost.

Playing Possum

Something was gnawing at my dream
and, awake now, I hear one of our cats
loudly crunching at his bowl in the kitchen.
But here in bed I make out the shapes
of all three cats, a triumvirate
around my wife and me. I leap up
through the question of *Something wrong,
honey?* and stumble toward the mad
chewing. I flick on the light. There,
in the corner, pink as a piglet, a baby
possum startles from the bowl of Kitten
Kaboodle, crumbs flaking around its tiny
gash of mouth. And here's Linda,
fully awake now, too, with not only a broom
for her, but one for me. She flings me mine
like Ricky Nelson tossing John Wayne
his loop-handled carbine in *Rio Bravo*.
And we're shutting doors behind us
and opening doors to the outside world,
which clearly terrifies this arboreal
rodent who's little more than whiplash
tail and provisional hiss. He scampers
under the German Schrank. I take a couple
of swipes underneath and tease out
a dust-covered catnip toy, a disposable
Bic, and half of what might have been
a slice of Donato's (pepperoni). The possum
folds into itself like a fist. But Linda
is choking up and waving her broom, ready,
so I thwack the thing broadside. It skids out

like a top-ended puck to my wife, who swings—
her breasts jiggling wonderfully (did I mention
we're both bone naked?)—and I'm skating
toward the wide-open front door, this 2 a.m.
game of Possum Broomball almost fun now,
and whoosh the critter so hard it cartwheels
like a cartoon possum through a racket
of katydids and other night fiddlers
and lands like a wad of flubber on the lawn.
As it scampers off, Linda and I stand
on the front porch, victorious, holding
our brooms in the manner of American
Gothic. Our next-door neighbor Jaime,
home from the late shift, turns her blue
Toyota into the drive, fixing us
with headlights. *It's scary how seriously
these Worleys take their housecleaning*
she may be saying to herself, at which point
there's nothing left for us to do, but wave.

His Funeral

My father was finally unconfused,
the noose of Alzheimer's snapped.
Around him the malodorous roses
and long shafts of lilies.

I squeezed his shoulder, patted it
like the flank of a favorite dog.
I knew this was a dumb, sentimental
gesture. I didn't care.

My sister said—the whole room listening—
that our father had gone now
to a better place. The funeral home
claque nodded like breeze-bent stalks.

I wished for a long moment my sister
was right, but then two men came
and closed the light from him.
His new roof screwed tightly down,

I could still hear him say, *A better place,*
Joyce? Show me the evidence. The organ
shook down dust from the oak beams.
Joyce sang loudly along on the first hymn

with the few people who'd come. In my head
I sang "Don't Fence Me In." Dad told me
he'd hummed this when the gates
of Stalag XI-B were flung open

and he hobbled out on makeshift crutches.
He was headed back to Kansas, its glorious
dullness and flatness, bars of sunshine
in his father's field, the amazing grace

of wheat and wheat and wheat.

On My Deathbed

(a love poem)

Because it will be desperation's
greatest hour, I've been practicing
for the day I'm finally alone—
the last cold tray wheeled away,

the heart machine's blue blips pulsing,
my nose stuffed with tubes,
the respirator breathing for me
so my lungs can shut down slowly,

gradually board up shop . . .
I've been practicing to bring back
(below the clot of pink clouds
outside my last window) three men

and a small boy fishing, a full moon
bobbing like a cork in the water.
I will have my father reel his slack
line in again, laugh with the men

laughing at what they've become:
muddy cold husbands holding empty
stringers. And as my wrist fills with
the IV solution, I'll try to will

my dad to search through static
for a ball game floating in from somewhere,
miraculous, the radio again crackling
like a tiny fire; and with me in that room

will be a girl I loved, beyond sense
and understanding, who dared me
on the hottest day in July to slide
my crewcut through a wrought-iron railing,

my head growing tumescent in the heat
and stuck there until local firemen
and three high-school linemen pried me
loose. I'd do it again just to hear

Irene's sweet laughter trail off
like tiny bells down the street . . .
And in that room, sitting around me
on the hard bed, so close I can touch

them, will be Emily Dickinson,
Dostoevski, and Mark Twain launching
great halos of smoke. And because I am
rehearsing this moment before the instant

when *will* becomes artifact, I know
there will be stupendous snowflakes,
tumbling circus snowflakes that flitter
down to touch me, an exfoliation

I will lift through, then drift out
of the room. I'll rise in sunlight
until lightning flashes from every creek
in Kentucky, until, even higher,

your voice (wife, inveterate lover) spins out
and threads around me, a conjured net
holding me there, a last breath-beat,
while unimaginably far below

the waters of the earth roll out
their gorgeous blinding copper sheets.

Jeff Worley, a native Kansan, is the author of three chapbooks and four books of poetry—*The Only Time There Is*, which won the Mid-List Press first-book competition in 1995, *A Simple Human Motion, Happy Hour at the Two Keys Tavern*, which was named cowinner in the Society of Midland Authors Literary Competition and 2006 Kentucky Book of the Year in Poetry, and *Best to Keep Moving*.

Worley's poems have been published widely in literary magazines and journals, including the *Georgia Review*, the *New England Review, Shenandoah, DoubleTake*, the *Sewanee Review*, and the *Southern Review*. He was the winner of the *Atlanta Review*'s 2002 Grand Prize for the poem "His Funeral" (included here), and has received three Al Smith Fellowships from the Kentucky Arts Council and a National Endowment for the Arts Creative Writing Fellowship.

On his way to becoming a poet, Worley worked as an offset pressman, cab driver, folk singer, and university professor. He moved to Kentucky from Pennsylvania in 1986, and for the past twenty years has written feature articles for *Odyssey*, the University of Kentucky magazine for research and scholarship. He has served as editor of the magazine since 1997.

Worley recalls discovering the power of literature at age nine, reading *Tom Sawyer* in bed on a wintry Wichita night. "I was there, playing hooky with Tom, falling in love with Becky Thatcher, hanging out with Huck Finn in the graveyard, and running away to an island with Tom to become a pirate. Literature invited my imagination in, and I was hooked."

Poets that influenced Worley early on were E. E. Cummings, James Wright, William Stafford, Weldon Keys, Theodore Roethke, and his first poetry writing teacher—Michael Van Walleghen. "It became clear to me in this undergraduate class that poetry could be written in a down-to-earth, conversational style, that some of the strongest contemporary poems read like interesting, unpremeditated speech, and that you could write about the most personal subjects. Michael made it clear to us that the 'literary tradition' wasn't nearly as important as following language down the page to see where it wanted to take you."

On "His Funeral": "My father was badly wounded in southern France in World War II, captured, and spent the last five months of the war in a prisoner-of-war camp. This confinement was clearly a defining event in his life, as was, later, the confinement and baffling confusion of Alzheimer's disease, which finally took him. I wanted to somehow link these two events and also commemorate his funeral in Tucson in 2000."

JEFFREY
Skinner

b. 1948

Hey Nineteen

My hands poured acid down the blue walls
of the pool, while the rich wife inside tended to
who knows what—her elegant miseries, her African violets—
and the man of the house shattered clay discs
crossing the sun. "Hey nineteen!" my partner Ed
called up from a hissing cloud, "Where's
yer mind?" I stopped pouring and his face
stuck up out of the mist, furious and sour
at thirty-five, half a life gone
to seasonal work and a wife who pushed
him away, even on good nights. That day
lasted all summer, and I stayed inside
myself, a boarder in my parents' house,
scrambling eggs in the kitchen while Mother
ripped through her mysteries in the den.
There was a lost love involved, naturally,
and an old grammar-school friend who
turned up one night with a zig-zag scar
down his cheek, and a baggie of good dope.
We climbed the reservoir fence at midnight,
sat by a doubled moon at the lake's shore
and talked like Chinese poets till dawn.
We agreed that rebirth gets tiresome, even
within one life, and that the brain
is sad and lonesome up in its tower,
connected to the mainland by cables only.
Vietnam was one senior year away, or Canada,
or Sweden; a savage tender marriage
five years away, and the idiot's discovery
that literature would not save me

ten years or more. But at nineteen you can work
without sleep, you can dream without sleep,
and I rode the pick-up to the next dry pool
in Greenwich strangely happy, Flaubert
tucked in my back pocket for reading on breaks
while Ed sat and smoked, staring at the rich man's
slate roof, the wavering aura of noon heat.

Uncle Joe

Said he knew the farmer so we could shoot
in his fields. I don't know caliber but the gun
seemed taller than me. First round went well—I blew
the beer can off the stump. He said you're
okay, kid. But the next time I relaxed and the butt
slipped from my shoulder. That crack was louder,
the scope kicked back, cut a red half moon
in my forehead. Jesus, he said. I didn't know
until my hand came away sticky and wet. He swept
me up and ran to the farmhouse. The farmer's wife
wore an apron like the forties had never gone.
She cleaned the wound and pulled the skin
together with a white butterfly. Only
then did my fear break open. I cried like
an idiot. She said if that's the worst thing
ever happens to you you'll be the luckiest
little man on earth. The truck cab stayed quiet
on the way home, Joe probably thinking Christ,
Doris'll be ticked. I remember turning that woman
over in my head, her words. What was the rest
of my life that she could say such a thing so calmly?

The School of Continuing Education

One day I saw four pines guarding a hill at dusk
and the hill was grassy so each shadow
from the pines made an only slightly darker green
oblong stretching down the hill in weak sun

and I said to myself I don't want to write
anymore I want to paint, writing
is inadequate finally to the look of things
and surrounded besides by all manner of yakking

equivocation and the money I've made from writing
total wouldn't cover the down payment
on the Levitt house my father bought in 1956
and what kind of unaffordable grand prize is *that*

so I took a beginning class in drawing
where to my amazement right away this naked woman
appeared on a sort of platform with klieg lights
throwing the crisp shadows of her breasts

here and there depending on the pose
and your point of view and we got to look
her up and down for three hours twice a week
I know what you're thinking but after mere minutes

it wasn't sexual at all really it was some sort
of clumsy meditation on the relation of various forms
of carbon-based matter: eye, vine-charcoal, paper,
hand, naked woman, and most of the time

the result was a million miles from her
who lay almost within range of our forbidden touch
amid mismatched pillows, languid and wisely incurious
about our wordless chorus of scritches

and really I did learn to draw somewhat
like a giant holding an eyebrow pencil
but not enough like a child to get serious, I admit
relief when the class ended and I went home

my wife said well are you done with all that
yes I said and didn't draw or write but cupped her breast
and the shadow of her breast together remembering
the pines and the shadows down the grassy hill

only a slightly darker green and then with our hips
and tongues and hands and that discreet officiate the soul
began the only making that is not shadow to
another, and for a moment we could see in the dark

Prodigal

There's no use, I guess, lamenting our interest
in Things Lost, Things We Have Not, But Want.
Shadows and erasures are interesting for what
they might contain: some range of movement
recalled, the face of a suicide friend, maybe.
But what we have now our eyes scan quickly
without register. Mike, the guy who works
at the bookstore, has a wooden prosthesis
for a left hand, and you want to say Hey
Mike, *what the hell happened to your hand?!*—
Because you have to forcibly hold your eye
back from that polished piece of wood, it's very
interesting. Instead you say Mike, you lazy
bastard, you were late opening up
Sunday morning, I owe you for a *Times*
I slipped out of the stack. Thank God for honest
thieves, Mike says. He's gentle but sardonic.
Money and beauty are interesting: nobody
has enough of either. The old woman wants to be
professionally made up in her hospital bed
before visitors arrive. The contorted distance
in her face as she weeps into the mirror
mimes the drama of final act revelation. But
when we've seen her snap the mirror shut
we're ready to move on. Restlessness is a sign
of intelligence, someone said, and evolution
bears this out: way back it paid to keep
one eye on the horizon for subtle spikes
in color, movement: predators. —The taste
for novelty passed on by those alert

enough not to become dinner. And stories
about journeys are just so much *better*
than stories about people sitting still. Never mind
we are advised by spiritual virtuosi to quiet
down, to Want What We Have. The hero
must move! Some piece of the human is missing
and odds are we did not leave it in some well-
lit room, tv splashing out its candy-colored
fountain, the sweet hammer of booze
within easy reach. No. What we want to see
again is the rich child who leaves,
who blows his inheritance on one silky
toy of the flesh after another, who sinks down
covered in the detritus of his own
delicious sin, grubbing with the pigs for a few
still-attached kernels of rotten corn.
Then, it's all erased. The child feels himself
without form and substance, having found
the white center of shadow. Hey Mike (Jim, Danny,
Paul)!, we want to say, What the hell happened
to *you!* But he doesn't recognize his name,
this rising pile of animate filth. Cloudless
heat. The flies, etc. The mountains wavering
like green scones far away. Tang of sulphurous air.
The son dragged home without a name.

Hard Labor

Such a long labor, my father's dying.
A long time to give birth to his own death.
The due date has passed, and still no sign of delivery.
Shriven muscles. Anvil head, impossible to lift

from the pillow. Nether end diapered and forlorn.
And yet his eyes open on a new light
pushing across the ceiling each morning, and close
on newer darkness pushing that. For me too

it's work: giving birth to my father's death.
I'm out in the streets daily, asking for sympathy,
lugging my puppet theater. But what can anyone,
you know, do? Two songs rail in my heart:

"Do Not Go Gentle," and "Deliver Your Death."
What will this child look like, when it comes?
When the issue of my father's death is born, the body
cleansed? Will it have my eyes? Call me daddy?

An English professor at the University of Louisville, **Jeffrey Skinner** has published five books of poetry—*Late Stars, A Guide to Forgetting* (a winner in the 1987 National Poetry series, chosen by Tess Gallagher), *The Company of Heaven, Gender Studies,* and *Salt Water Amnesia*. He has edited two anthologies of poems, *Last Call: Poems of Alcoholism, Addiction, and Deliverance* and *Passing the Word: Poets and Their Mentors.* Skinner is also a playwright—his play *Dream On* premiered in 2007 in Philadelphia.

Skinner's poems have appeared in the most prestigious magazines in this country, including the *New Yorker,* the *Atlantic,* the *Nation,* the *American Poetry Review, Poetry,* the *Georgia Review,* and the *Paris Review.* His poems, plays, and stories have won grants, fellowships, and awards from the National Endowment for the Arts, the Ingram Merrill Foundation, the Howard Foundation, and the state arts agencies of Connecticut, Delaware, and Kentucky. Skinner is president of the board of directors and editorial consultant for Sarabande Books, a literary publishing house he founded with his wife, the poet Sarah Gorham.

Skinner was born in Buffalo, New York, and grew up during a time, he says, when "your mom let you out in the morning and expected you home for dinner, and you were free to roam, to get lost." He loved reading (Kipling, Poe, Sherlock Holmes) and loved "pretend adventures." "I remember wanting to be Mowgli [in *The Jungle Book*] very badly, and believing with all my heart that the apple tree in our yard was the entrance to the jungle; and there I climbed to become Mowgli. But also I wanted to be a soldier, a cowboy, the fastest runner in the world. And so I was. We lived and played comfortably within the imagination."

On his way to becoming a poet, Skinner worked as a swimming pool cleaner, private investigator, psychiatric aide, actor, and research psychologist. His life as a poet was triggered by a book he discovered after his college days, *Writings to an Unfinished Accompaniment* by W. S. Merwin. "I thought, you can *do* this with language? It's *permitted*? Then I was off reading every book of contemporary poetry I could lay my hands on."

On "Hard Labor": "I wrote this poem after my father died in 2004. It came at the end of a suite of poems in which he appeared as a dream figure, a kind of fairytale presence, able to shift shape and identity. The poems were catharsis, and they also allowed me to understand my mourning in the only terms that I, in the end, trusted: language. This experience made clearer than ever my reliance on poetry as a way of seeing and understanding reality. My father's death was protracted and hard to watch; it was a 'difficult birth.' I see my love for him reflected in the poem's rigor and wryness, and I am glad."

GEORGE ELLA Lyon

b. 1949

My Grandfather in Search of Moonshine

For once he wanted
some high quality white
to keep on the pantry shelf
back behind beans and corn
to reach for and apply
whenever the wound came open.
So he asked his brother-in-law, Jim,
what door he should knock on.
Jim sent him up the creek.
He'd hardly got his feet set
for climbing that rooty staircase
when he met a stranger coming down,
beard thick and under his arm
a shoebox tied with twine.

"Evening, I'm looking for some moonshine.
You know of any up this way?"
"Don't know as I do." He pulled at his beard.
"But five dollars might find some."
The bill passed.
The man handed him the box.
"Wait here, and hold these shoes."

He waited. He walked, whistled, chewed
spat grasshoppers off stones.
Quarter hour passed, then half,
earthclock winding its shadows:
no grisly man, no jar
with its creekwater turned to song.
He felt anger under his ribs,

fire at the edge of a field.
He cursed, kicked rocks,
wiped fool-sweat from his face.
"Least I've got his shoes," he thought.
"That's something, if they fit."
He cut the twine with his pocket knife,
lifted the dusty lid. There was his jar.
"I'll be damned," he said,
opened it and drank,
turning like a twig on a spider strand
hung plumb-bob for the web.

Mother's Day at the Air Force Museum

1.
My husband and son go before me
through the chill of May
to look at bombers.
Another woman, pregnant,
climbs the stairs behind me
up to the opened cockpit.

Signs label these planes
outmoded, inefficient.
The woman behind me sweats.
It still takes nine months
to build a child.

2.
My son loves the machine guns.
He looks through a sight,
he strafes the still air.
At home, his Lego men
die smiling.

This is our history, I tell myself.
Pay attention.

In uniform, boys
become men. In uniform,
we become women.
Tight military coat
Loose maternity shirt

We fill the bowl
               they eat
we fill the crib
we protect the baby's head
in the soft blue hood
until he climbs into a plane
pregnant with death.

3.
Reading the walls, I learn
how little time it took
after finding flight
to fit the guns on the wings.
A brief tour of the sky
and we arrive at atomic bombs.
The pregnant woman rests
in a plastic chair.

4.
The last display is a recording
of Mrs. John Magee
reading "High Flight"
the sonnet her son wrote
before he died at 19.

Beside the text are telegrams
the Royal Canadian Air Force
sent to his father.

His mother carves the air
with her voice, holding his poem

against the folded flag,
the plaque in an unknown church.

She sees him pull up
take his fierce steps
her hand between his head
and where he might fall.

Salvation

What does the Lord want with Virgil's heart?
And what is Virgil going to do without one?

O Lord, spare him the Call.
You're looking for bass
in a pond stocked with catfish.
Pass him by.
You got our best.
You took Mammy and the truck and the second hay.
What do You want with Virgil's heart?

Virgil, he comes in of a night
so wore out he can hardly chew
blacked with dust that don't come off at the bathhouse.
He washes again
eats onions and beans with the rest of us
then gives the least one a shoulder ride to bed
slow and singing
> *Down in some lone valley*
> *in some lonesome place*
> *where the wild birds do whistle . . .*

After that, he sags like a full feed sack
on a couch alongside the TV
and watches whatever news Your waves are giving.
His soul sifts out
like feed from a slit in that sack
and he's gone
wore out and give out and plumb used up, Lord.
What do you want with his heart?

Catechisms

*—poem found in conversations
with a four-year-old*

What's the oldest thing that's living?
> Trees probably — California redwoods.

I mean that moves around.
> A tortoise I guess.

No, I mean that moves around and talks:
the oldest thing.
> Some person somewhere.

Are your bones going to come through?
> What?

When your sunburn peels, are your bones
going to poke through?
> No, no, there's new skin under there.
> It's tough.

Will they ever?
> Not unless I get a bad break.

Don't do that.
> No.

They'd have to put you in the hard stuff.
> What?

The white bone stuff. They'd have to put it
all over.
> That's called a cast.

Do they sew bones?
> No, bones can grow back together.

Who will die first?

George Ella Lyon is one of the most visible and active poets in Kentucky, appearing in the past twenty-five years at hundreds of schools as a visiting author and teaching regularly in community workshops such as the Appalachian Writers Workshop, Hindman Settlement School, and the Writer's Voice program at Lexington's Carnegie Center, where she has served as writer-in-residence. She has also conducted dozens of workshops for teachers and librarians in the United States and Germany.

Born and raised in Harlan County in the mountains of Kentucky, she has published two collections of poems (*Mountain* and *Catalpa,* winner of the Appalachian Book of the Year Award), a novel (*With a Hammer for My Heart*), a book of short fiction (*Choices*), twenty-two picture books and five novels for young readers (including *Borrowed Children,* winner of the Golden Kite Award), and an autobiography (*A Wordful Child*). She recently edited the anthology *A Kentucky Christmas* (University Press of Kentucky). *Where I'm From: Where Poems Come From,* an engaging and accessible text on how to write poetry, is a favorite of teachers statewide.

Both of her parents were avid readers, Lyon says, and she recalls her father reading aloud to her from *A Hundred and One Famous Poems.* "I was especially drawn to Millay, Dickinson, and Edgar Lee Masters. In sixth grade, I read Hopkins's 'Spring and Fall,' and it hit me so hard I thought I was getting the flu!" Later, as a student at Centre College in Danville, she "fell," she says, for Yeats and Ferlinghetti.

On "Catechisms": "This poem came from three conversations I had with my son, Benn, when he was four. All the questions in the poem are questions he asked over a three-week period. It wasn't until he got to 'Who will die first?' that I realized this question underscored his concern from the beginning. I found this very sad and cosmic. But when I told Benn it was unlikely that both his dad and I would die at the same time, he breathed a sigh of relief and said, 'Then there'll still be somebody to get me some orange juice.' This gave me another perspective."

LEATHA
Kendrick

b. 1949

Wedding Album

And it's this photo of her reaching out, my mother
reaching out to touch my veil, that always holds me.

She sent the first two fingers of her left hand
to the lace edge, and I remember the man

we'd known for years by his first name, the hometown
photographer who posed us to act as if

she arranged the voile along my cheek. Another act
artificial, uncertain, like so much in those winter weeks—

picking out the blue china, the off-white,
high-necked dress and the stephanotis trailing

from funereal stands. I posed. The gardenias, though,
we both wanted for my bouquet, almost the only thing

alive between us—their scent palpable
as the love we'd nearly forgotten to feel,

we'd grown so used to posing. So when he said
to pretend, she reached out and I looked into her eyes,

my smile tender, as if we shared something
private. I saw her gaze drop, saw what

almost welled up, and I wanted to lean in, to embrace her,
but it wasn't the pose we were supposed to strike.

Refusing a Spinal

Six years old and pale that night, I was already experienced
in surgery—days in my father's clinic,
evenings when he let me ride along.
This night the cow stood quiet,
straining and her backside bulging as if to split. I screeched,
"Something's wrong!" I knew something had to be
sideways when she hadn't waited for Dad to cut
the clean window in her side and pull out
the soaking calf and neatly sew the edges
like two halves of a blanket
hem-stitched. Not this mix
of shit and straw, cobwebs greasy with old dust
the one raw bulb hanging brown
with fly droppings, her baby falling finally
onto the slime.

                                    No wonder
the doctor said to me twenty-one years later
when I requested natural childbirth
(me in the chair and him behind the square
expanse of desk in the right
angles of his well-lit office, walls
blazing with white rectangles)—no wonder
he said to me that he could not understand
why some women wanted to have their babies
like cows in a barn. It was then
I saw again the liquid gleaming
globe of the cow's eye, the patient
rhythm squeezing her sides, the calm
heaving and the pale tips

of the calf's hoofs tender as tulips
as he left her, the swell
and rush of water, the newborn swimming
out into the half-dark of the barn.

                                    I could not speak
in that white room, was sobbing so hard as I left
that my friend had to ask, "What's wrong? Did the baby die?"
I could see my father watching from the shadows,
hear the rough scraping of the cow's tongue,
regular as a heart urging the newborn
onto his feet, her sudden lowing,
so loud it startled me. My father
loved to blast our ignorance, loved to laugh
at any fear whiting our eyes. Running
his hand along the sharp ridge of her spine,
he said, "*This* is how things get born."

Second Opinion

We're four women waiting among a shifting set of others
in radiology's store-front lobby—three daughters
and a mother linked by blood and laughter
over *Cosmo Girl*'s "most embarrassing
moments" (trail of toilet paper from the back of slacks,
the inevitable period started when you're wearing white,
a student asking her teacher, "If your quizzies are hard,
what about your testes?") Lyda loves that last one—
my funny last one—she's the performer, the mime.
Thank god, she's mine, feeding me one-liners.

The middle one, Eliza, brought my x-rays here,
and parked the car. She works the crossword,
all attention like her father but she's part of me,
my watching self. And Leslie, eldest, watches over us all,
rails against this three hour wait, tries to breach
the impersonal walls of disinterest in our fate. She was first
to nurse from this right breast, that pressed and prodded,
and later slicked with gel will echo sound onto a screen
to show the probable malignancy. I'm going to lose it—

the breast—and along with it the cancer, too, I hope.
The receptionist gives us a hard look when we laugh.
We're linked, silvery with a happiness
glinting out even in this waiting place.
I finger the necklace I've just bought, touch
the curative moonstone, murmuring "hope"—
I want to believe in sudden remission,
in some way to avert what we are certainly
headed for. What I can believe in
is the healing of their fingers laced through mine.

Costume. Fakery. The Sell.

On watching TV two weeks post-mastectomy

Excuse me while I grow bald and fat.
Sorry to offend the eye with my
one breast. I'm female. I apologize.
I fake two breasts, but know this half-flat
chest. I'll take chemo and a wig,
touch my losses secretly. No big
deal! I never have and never will
fit anyone's ideal. And I'm no star-
fish: won't regenerate. Fiberfill
and silicone help to hide the scar.
This new shape won't fill t-shirts, sell a car.
I'm served up on the half-shell. Turn off
the TV. Its cleavage shouts, "Are you buying?"
Avert your eyes. I've one soft side. I'm off
the market. Alive! Tender, I'm not hiding.

In Passing

Look, I know the moon
stares down through tonight's
blowing snow grains like time

won't end. I know the snow
itself stays as long as
the cold lasts. I know that

seems like forever,
the way summer, stuck
on the long ledge of a July

afternoon, feels as if it cannot
fall—but I don't have much
time and such illusions

of endless anything I
still harbor arrive
pinched flat in an envelope.

I don't have so much
as a nickel's worth
of advice to spend on you

or on anyone, now death's
resident already
in my flesh, insisting

on her solid, if misshapen,
reality. I've got to say
only what is necessary,

things like, What a meal
that was! How's the wife
been feeling? Isn't this
a gorgeous day?

Born in Granite City, Illinois, **Leatha Kendrick** was raised in Franklin, Kentucky, where most of her father's family lived. As the child of a Yankee/Dixie, Republican/Democrat marriage, she claims to be a "northern Southern" poet, belonging to both the red-clay South and the black-loam Midwest. "Because of my background," she says, "I'm attuned to fields and fences, to divisions and boundaries, to dialects and accents, to the dirt of two regions."

Kendrick has published three collections of poems—*Second Opinion, Science in Your Own Back Yard,* and *Heart Cake*—and coedited, with George Ella Lyon, the anthology *Crossing Troublesome: Twenty-Five Years of the Appalachian Writers Workshop.* Her poems and essays have appeared in the *Louisville Review, Shenandoah, Connecticut Review, Nimrod,* and other periodicals, and her work has been included in *The Kentucky Anthology, Listen Here: Women Writing in Appalachia,* and *A Kentucky Christmas.*

Kendrick's writing awards include two Al Smith Fellowships from the Kentucky Arts Council, the Jim Wayne Miller Poetry Prize, and residencies at the Hambidge Center for the Creative Arts, the Vermont Studio Center, and the Mary Anderson Center for the Creative Arts. Currently director of the New Books by Great Writers reading series at the Carnegie Center for Literacy and Learning in Lexington, she has taught at the University of Kentucky, Morehead State University, and Prestonsburg Community College.

In high school, Kendrick was impressed with the poetry of Dylan Thomas and Tennyson ("the sound!"), and among contemporary poets was "hugely influenced" by James Wright, Molly Peacock, Sydney Lea, and Mark Cox.

On "Refusing a Spinal": "This poem was a long time coming—more than twenty years between the triggering event and finding a way to talk about it. I could finally write this poem after I realized that not everyone experienced what I did growing up with a veterinarian father, who expected us all to lend a hand at whatever work needed to be done at the moment—from delivering calves to setting tobacco. Though the images of the poem embedded themselves in me at the doctor's office, as I describe, I had to grow into the craft and courage that allowed me to put them in a poem. I believe courage and craft are intertwined. As I experienced the discipline of writing and paid attention to craft, I found that I could make a container for emotions I had not been able to express before. The line breaks and white spaces allowed me to find the rhythm of the experience and to hear its music. The poem, as a 'made thing,' can have a beauty and orderliness that the experience did not have."

MAX
Garland

b. 1950

Hold on Me

The year I turned twelve I thought love
lived in the blond straw of the manger,
the naked face of the moon,
and AM rock and roll—

four-beat bass line, embellishing
waves of doo-wop, the brutal equation,
of say, the *Miracles* singing—

You treat me badly,
I love you madly,

which made sense to a Methodist,
for wasn't life an earthly penance
for the faithlessness of angels—
fallen apples of God's just eye?
And wasn't that Jesus, stapled
to the hilltop, his broken heart,
our valentine?

The year I was twelve, the stilted
grammar of greeting cards was love.
If you could just nail the rhyme scheme,
wouldn't human sympathy follow?

In other words, I knew nothing,
except crescendos and the closing
credits of movies felt like love,

and the way animals looked at you,
and that cut grass smelled
like what the word *unrequited*
would someday come to mean.

I lined my mother's lipsticks up
like so many beautiful bullets.
I'd never tasted a single kiss,
though I imagined one
hot as a wound.

. . . don't like you,
but I love you,

or some such anthem,
crackled along the household air,
the year I was twelve.

Love was a brave little racket.

Through the back of the kitchen radio,
you could see it
in the glowing vacuum tube,
like a tiny bush that burned inside,
commanding the static to sing.

Requiem for a Boom Town

It was Sunday, 1957, and the parking lot
of the Episcopal Church
was the best time a tail-fin ever had.

The sunlight fractured itself, car after car,
each one sleeker than the one before;
cars the size of small living rooms,
each one more radiant;

as if the families merely waited
in the church, killing time,
while the real worship
was parked in the lot,

was the sun on the grillwork, or shapely
along the fenders,

or in the names of the animals
emblazoned above the trunk latches.

The real worship was in the sound
of the car door closing, heavy
as a vault, the settling in,
and that moment of silence
just before he turned her over,

and felt himself, the wife, the son,
the daughter, lifted in the glittering wave
of all a man could ever want.

The Termite Confessions

It wasn't the worst job I'd had, wasn't
sweeping parking lots, or sponging toilets,
wasn't digging graves in packed clay.
But it was crawling in the dark
beneath houses, through generations
of cobwebs, cast-off snake skins,
brick shards, with my flashlight
and termite hammer, tapping for rot,
for the crumble of wood that meant
they were there, legions of them—
insatiable nymphs, blind white workers;
while above me the house sagged,
the duct-work flexed, the worried owner
scraped a kitchen chair across linoleum
as I inched my way along, belly-up
in the realm of the tiny beasts
tunneling themselves into the galleries
of the floorboards, mining the wood
for cellulose, sucking it out like honey
until even the oak grew papery,
dry as puffball,

and eventually drew the house down,
though it could take a century or two.
Time is on the side of appetite,
I found myself deciding; and maybe
it was the damp, the must, the mold,
the torn scarves of spiderwebs I wore,
but I felt in strange cahoots,
noticed a pull as I crawled

under the nail heads and grouted pipes.
Sometimes even switched off the light
and just lay beneath a riddled beam
and felt myself crossing over,
the way secret agents must feel
in the arms of their informants,
or even the best executioners
eventually come to feel—that shift
in perspective, allegiance,
as if some small dark love
were gnawing its way inside,
and the last thing I wanted
was light.

For a Johnson County Snowfall

I'd settle for a paradise like this,
that kept falling apart
and regathering, that slowed
time, faltered
and hung like the weight of grace
on the houses.

I'd settle for a paradise
that folded like a white book
over the scrawl of underbrush
and twigs, that simplified
the landscape, absolving
the roads of destination.

A few birds tag along
in a rich, grey wind.
The trees are pared
to a minimal faith.

Isn't there already a place
where *blessing* and *snow*
are the same word?

I'd settle for such a paradise,
that you could gather by the handful,
though it might soon begin to burn
with the same cold knack
the winter stars have.

I'd settle for a paradise
that could be fashioned into a man,
however temporary, or comical:
a cocked hat, a pair
of ordinary stones for his eyes;
a paradise that nevertheless
could spread its spindly arms
as wide as the night was bitter,
as the wind was ice, and whirled,
and swept, and sang like a blade.

A professor of English at the University of Wisconsin–Eau Claire, Kentucky native **Max Garland** is the author of two books of poetry—*Hunger Wide as Heaven* and *The Postal Confessions*, which won the Juniper Prize for Poetry in 1995. His poems, fiction, and essays have been published in *Chicago Review,* the *Georgia Review,* the *Gettysburg Review,* the *Iowa Review,* and *Poetry,* among others. His poem "Because You Left Me a Handful of Daffodils" was read by Garrison Keillor on National Public Radio's *The Writer's Almanac* and was also chosen by Billy Collins for the anthology *Poetry 180: A Poem a Day for American High Schools.*

Among his many honors and awards are a Wisconsin Arts Board Artist Fellowship for Poetry, a Bush Foundation Artist Fellowship Award, a James Michener/Copernicus Society of American Fiction Fellowship Award, and a National Endowment for the Arts Poetry Fellowship.

Garland, who holds an M.F.A. in creative writing from the University of Iowa, says that growing up in Paducah in the 1950s and early 1960s had almost everything to do with his poetry. "Living on the Ohio River—that border between North and South, between one accent and another, one history and another—is something that surfaces in poem after poem." He adds that various jobs he had have also influenced his writing. Before leaving Kentucky in 1990 for an academic career, Garland worked as a paperboy, grocery clerk, recreation supervisor, nursery worker, ice cream truck driver, pizza cook, termite inspector, janitor, and rural mail carrier. "The rural mail carrier job was probably the most significant, since for almost ten years I ran the same rural route my grandfather had run for twenty-five years before me, the route on which I was born and where most of my relatives lived. It stretched about twenty-five or thirty miles, much of it along the Ohio River in western Kentucky."

Garland says his early literary influences include the King James Bible ("one of the only books in our house"), 1960s folk music lyrics, and the English Romantics. He most admires, among modern poets, William Stafford, for the voice and range of his work.

MARCIA
Hurlow

b. 1952

Aliens Are Intercepting My Brain Waves

This eggplant glistens, purple satin.
The tomatoes, the grapefruit, the unripe
bananas gather beautifully in my cart.
But the Star captures my thoughts:
a woman just like me is feeding
secrets to space aliens. She can't help it.
They're intercepting her brain waves
from their rocket on Venus.
She can't sleep for fear of what her dreams
might reveal. Every day her brain waves
grow weaker. She looks like the living dead.

The *Enquirer* reports on twin girls
in the jungle of Brazil. Blind, speechless,
they play their sibling games by brain waves.
There are photos: the girls dress in skins
of giant otters, big as a man. They stand
in tall grass, holding hands and offering
me tropical flowers, petals long and thick
as hot dogs. Investigators found that
Etana and Emara taught each other
the constellations, predicted eclipses
and the phases of the moon.

Last night the quarter moon was dim
when Joe and I walked home from Mother's.
He said old hippies believe the shimmering
lights on Mt. Shasta are aliens working,
planning. Maybe, I thought, it's gas
or car lights from I-5 caught

on the mica and quartz. He said some force
draws people to that dead volcano, and soon
it will explode, the head of a circle
of fire, and every star will turn black.

Then we saw a flash through the sky, a shape
with two lights, dull yellow, pinned
to the tips of its wings. "Aliens,"
he insisted. "Don't say anything else.
Draw what you saw, real
careful. First thing tomorrow we'll compare
my sketch with yours, see what that thing was."
I drew with skill, with accuracy I'd never had.
Every color and curve came as clearly as if
I had been at the cold, silvery field
when the two crewmen boarded. Velvety
stairs rolled up behind them and they left
me behind. Sometime before dawn I knew

It was a trick. How many illusions
does it take to make the truth? Somehow,
Joe, my dominant twin, had told me
what the spaceship looked like, what
to draw. In the morning paper was a photo
of the stealth bomber and an earlier
artist's rendering, probably closer to reality,
yes, surely, closer to what I had seen
than what Joe wanted me to draw. I copied it
carefully. At breakfast, in Joe's drawing
I saw the three spacemen beckon me aboard.

Margin of Loss

The Depression ate your coal-hauling business,
your contracting business; even your farms
languished. Your three small sons, one my father,
were always hungry.

                What would you do—never
something beyond our human nature. You found
a new use for your fields, the deep shelter
of chestnut trees, the long-bed trucks whose tires
were starting to rot.

                I can't imagine where you found
all the bottles, the jugs that began to fill
the corn bins and chicken houses. You knew
how to make connections, run a business
invisibly. You knew how to meet demands
and become nocturnal, detecting movement
without the need for sight.

                So one night
by the Kokosing River, waiting for the skiff
to take your load, you noticed the other car
sitting on the bank. The driver narrowed his eyes

to watch the stars slip out of the clouds.
Both of you saw that the ancient light revealed
nothing. You clutched your pistol, stepped
into sand and soap flowers.

                    At this bend
where the Kokosing broadens and slows, no music
of water rushing away distracted you. Here
in summers past, you taught each of your sons
to swim, tossing them into the deepest point
and turning your back. As a child you set
your lines here. No sunfish was too small
to skewer and fry.

                    The man in the dark
sedan told you he was waiting for sleep
to come, or a woman, or maybe a boat of his own,
but before you knew his name or his face, his hand
dipped beneath the shadowed seat and you
fired into the back of his head.

                                    You stayed
long enough to help the boatman stack the liquor
and to collect your money, long enough
for the sheriff to read, by the old moon
scything into dawn, your back license plate
jolting up to Route 229. Now forty years after
your death, your last living son tells me your
story days before surgery he may not survive.
I can't pretend my life will ever balance
this old debt or any other ledger.

The Pantheist Who Loved His Wife

Everyone knew that someone
had killed his wife,
someone had taken her
bright black hair, her small, thin bones
into the woods by the high school

and heaped them near the river
singing its sparks over black stones.
And there were flowers, tiny
white ones and violets he knew
better than to pick—they would be

limp, shriveled before she was
buried. He let police follow him
through fields and ravines, calling her
to call back from the earth. He knew
she was living everywhere now.

The Sisterhood

(Shakertown at Pleasant Hill, Kentucky)

Chaste women in long aprons
sorted the endless stream

of seed as their fingers
grew into knots.

They saved only the best,
and that they tucked

into square, colored packets
they sent into the world.

Virtuous women, they dreamed wild
trees roiling with Dutch designs.

Modest translators, they
taught each other to untangle

the bright embroidery left
on their doorsteps at dawn,

to sew it into the unknown
orchards of their sleep.

Dark brown, orange and gold
forms hung, moist and glowing

from the tree of life
that Sarah dreamed each night

for a week. In West Sisters House
she stitched those inviting

shapes, vague with waking,
and sang the songs of faith.

What if she were awakened
ten minutes sooner by

Brother Jacob's kiss—would she see
that those colored globes bore

wings and leaves, fins
and fountains, or would the tree

dissolve into Jacob's
brown eyes, bright wings of hair?

The Music of the Spiders

for Lawson Fusao Inada

Never mind why I have worked so late—
I put my head down on the table
to rest my eyes, when I see the spider,
a kleenex intaglio. I lift the edge
of the tissue to release him. He runs
like a night club singer to the spot
of light from my lamp. Then still. Is he
waiting for the band to begin? Then alive
with some inner trumpet, a luminous,
jazz-rhythm spider, frenetically blows
his cool lines, his silver licks, his spare
change high into shadow off-stage. Applaud
those jump-beat threads, those be-bop rays,
and oh, those sweet blue spaces in between.

Marcia Hurlow is a professor of English and journalism at Asbury College near Lexington, where she has taught since 1983. Her collections of poetry—*Aliens Are Intercepting My Brain Waves, Dangers of Travel, A Tree Ogham, Anomie,* and *Green Man in Suburbia*—all won book competitions. Her poems have appeared in more than 300 literary magazines, including *Poetry, Poetry Northwest, Poetry East, Chicago Review,* and *River Styx.* Hurlow holds a Ph.D. in rhetoric and applied linguistics from Ohio State University, and an M.F.A. in creative writing from Vermont College.

She grew up in Mt. Vernon, Ohio, in the backyard of Kenyon College, where, she says, "everyone was into poetry." Her earliest literary influences were Robert Louis Stevenson, whose poems her father helped her memorize before she could read. In high school, she discovered Theodore Roethke's poetry ("It was like candy, like music"), and the poets she currently most admires include Linda Pastan, Robert Frost, Gary Soto, Rita Dove, Jorie Graham, and Sharon Olds.

On "Margin of Loss": "This poem grew out of a scientific detail in an issue of the *Smithsonian* that caught my attention: your mother was giving you good advice to wear a hat when it's cold, because you lose the most body heat from the top of your head. That detail led me to others about loss in science and nature until I worked up enough steam to talk about other personal kinds of loss. Whoops! I wasn't ready after all. Sentimentality flooded my imagination, and when it stalls like that, I ask the reader to make the leap instead. No matter my grief *du jour,* the reader may be experiencing something worse. No matter the loss, the reader knows there is a thin margin of thought—as thin as the stretched latex of a balloon—that makes it bearable a little bit longer. In general, most of my poems come from a sound or phrase that intrigued me, so I follow it to see where it will go. Sometimes a poem comes from mentally arguing with another poem I've read, perhaps with content but more often an opportunity the poet missed."

FREDERICK
Smock

b. 1954

Heron

The blue heron has come to Franklin County,
to the topmost branches of a dead
cypress beside a pond on my friend Richard
Taylor's farm. We hiked up there with the dogs
the other day. Even the blind dog came along.
We clambered over slave walls, through
the high grass, to the top of the hill. The pond
shone like the eye of a cathedral dome, and
we gathered around it, almost touching the heavens.
There the cypress, her nest big as a sombrero.
The valley lay below us, checkered in greens—
the palisades of the Elkhorn rose up in the east,
the skies led away to far blue horizons.
Somewhere out there, heron was unfolding her
long pale wings. We knew because
the blind dog kept looking in the same direction.

Homeward

Our car stuck deep in a snowbank,
we set out walking toward the yellow light
of a farmhouse several fields away.
We jumped a creek, and climbed a fence.
In the middle field, a horse approached us,
nodding and nodding her slow sweet head,
as if she saw our trouble and what we needed
to make it right. We stood in the hot circle
of her breath, stroking her long sleek nose,
warming our hands. We breathed in the hay-
barn scent of her skin. We ran our palms
over her withers, a broad smooth run
like a ski-trail high on a mountain ridge,
the snow we needed to carry us homeward.

Poem for Cassius Clay

My father used to work
in Cassius Clay's corner,
and he said to him one night,
"My son would like to meet you,"
and Cassius laughed a big horse-laugh,
and put his big brown hand on
my shoulder, weighted me down
with it, he did, and I slumped
under his beauty, and his anger,
and I carried the weight of
his big hand away with me
that night on my shoulder
like a chip looking to get
knocked off.

On the Gold Medal That Lies at the Bottom of the Ohio River

1960

Cassius Clay had just returned from
his Olympic boxing conquest in Rome,
where he had also shadow-boxed
on the Via Veneto for the passersby
(a painter goes to Italy for the light,
a boxer for the exquisite shadow).
Still wearing his gold medal on his neck,
he walked into a white diner in Louisville
for a bite to eat and he was refused.
He brandished his gold medal
and told the counterman *who he was.*
It made no difference. Thrown out,
his heart a big black cinder in his chest.
It made him crazy mad. He wandered
up onto the Second Street bridge,
and he threw his gold medal into
the muddy Ohio River.

1988

I took my son up onto the bridge,
and there I told him this story.
It is a famous story, locally.
I had wanted my telling of it to be
about racism, not violence,
although the two are blood brothers.
Anyway, I told him the story.

He was quiet for a moment after,
staring into the swirling brown water,
then he asked if I thought Cassius Clay
ever wanted his gold medal back again.
I don't know, I said, *I don't know.*
Maybe now that gold medal lies
submerged in my son's consciousness,
gleaming small and distant.
Maybe it has sunk out of memory.
Maybe it will resurface as a goldfish
in another story altogether,
one that my son tells me.

Born and raised in Louisville, **Frederick Smock** is a professor and chairman of the Department of English at Bellarmine University, where he also directs the creative writing program. He has published seven collections of poems, a collection of essays (*Poetry & Compassion: Essays on Art & Craft*), a critical study of Thomas Merton (*Pax Intrantibus: A Meditation on the Poetry of Thomas Merton*), and a travel memoir. Smock has also edited *The American Voice Anthology of Poetry.*

His poems and essays have been published in the *Iowa Review, Poetry, Shenandoah,* the *Southern Review,* and the *Writer's Chronicle.* In addition to his life as a poet and essayist, Smock has served as a book critic for the *Louisville Courier-Journal* since 1980 and was editor in chief of the *American Voice,* an international literary journal, from 1984 to 1999. His honors and awards include an Al Smith Fellowship in Poetry from the Kentucky Arts Council, the Henry Leadingham Poetry Prize, and the Jim Wayne Miller Prize for Poetry.

Smock counts himself lucky to have discovered Jane Kenyon's poetry early on and also admires the work of Jack Gilbert, Wendell Berry, Robert Hass, and Mary Oliver. These writers, he says, "know and have the talent to practice the secret to writing—the right word in the right place every time." And speaking of place, Smock adds that he has always felt very rooted in Louisville, where he currently lives. "This rootedness has helped to define me and to free me to write *from* this place if not always *of* this place."

On "Poem for Cassius Clay": "My father, a young medical intern, was Muhammad Ali's doctor, back when Ali was an amateur called Cassius Clay. My father used to take me with him to the fights at the Armory on Saturday nights. While he did his doctoring, I wandered around between the rings, where amateurs of every stripe fought their bouts. I wandered around among gamblers, promoters, pimps, prostitutes, hustlers—the fight crowd in Louisville in the '50s. Me, a kid in blue shorts and a white button-down Oxford-cloth shirt. This went on until the night my mother detected, upon my return home, that my shirt was minutely flecked with blood. I count myself lucky, in my poems about Ali, to have found a bit of language to describe his power of personality."

ALEDA
Shirley

1955–2008

My Parents When They Were Young

Sleet whips the trees against the house
and pushes clouds across the sky. Or maybe
it's the sky moving behind clouds:
for that's the way I've begun to feel age,
something absolute shifting behind days
of sunlight, days of snow.
Snug in its brown skin, the turkey
smells of sage; the cranberry sauce glimmers
like a big fake jewel in the revere bowl.
And my father, leaning
against the gray window, muses how
when I was seven, he was the age I am now;
my mother tips forward in her rocker and asks
if I remember them when they were young.

And I try to erase the definition
of smile and frown in her face,
to pluck out the salt strands
in his salt-and-pepper hair, to remember
when they were the grown-ups and late at night
was a place they went without me:
if I could see them walking, hand in hand,
around the square in Murfreesboro
as dusk trembled on their shoulders
and the courthouse crept off into darkness
and the movie marquee lit up . . . but I am a child,
insinuating myself into this scene,
crying, from a sitter's porch,
Come back, come back.

They are asking me to remember
because they are afraid of dying.
I want to whisper: I know, I know—
you read me a story and I fought sleep,
I wanted the tale to go on forever;
you carried me in from the car
in the middle of the night and went back out
in the rain to get my doll or the moon,
whatever it was I'd left on the backseat.
Do I tell them how some physicists believe
that on the subatomic level time may move
in both directions? Only the sea can remember
everywhere it's been, and we'll have
between us always those twenty-odd years.

One Summer Night

The sherbet-colored lawn chairs arranged
themselves in pairs, like dancers,
and my grandfather rattled his newspaper,
cigarette smoke curling like a bad mood around him.
This was how it was twenty years ago
in Oakland, Kentucky: my uncles telling jokes
as they took turns turning the ice cream freezer,
my grandmother drying her hands on her apron
and, there, by the door, my mother talking softly
to her sisters about a time longer ago than this one
I long for. Slow, like a slow dance:
my cousins and I waded through green shadows
and touched the tips of honeysuckle
to the tips of our tongues. The walnut,
heavy with fruit, was a ship with tall pink sails,
the patio a kind of shore and the adults calling
Girls, ice cream the light of a lighthouse
beaming across dark distance. Night fell
gently as if it were bending down to look
in our faces; waving sparklers
we filled the air with rhinestones, so profuse
and lovely they had to be fake.

Odd now to think no one had walked
on that moon rising in the mimosa's shallow limbs
and odd to understand how, more than that night, I want
to know they want it back as much as I do. For this
I would forfeit my dozen cities, even the loveliest one;
the thin clear goodnight the child calls
from across the street; my lover's hands

on my upper arms as he rises above me in the dark.
I'd give up the secrets I've coaxed from memory's
closed fist and the ability to articulate them.
Though not the desire.

Hostage to Fortune

Often, when you're away on business, I wake
in the middle of the night with something
urgent or whimsical to tell you
and then, the next morning,
can't remember what it was. And sometimes
I bring in your khakis and oxford cloth shirts,
your socks and underwear,
and pile them, still warm from the dryer, on the bed.
I pull a cuff across my arm and watch
static crackle the hair on my wrist.
When I take a shower
steam brings out the ghost of the aftershave
you put on earlier in the day and for a second,
forgetting, I peer out the shower curtain
to see if you're there.

How fragile your plane would seem
if I stood on the beach where I once lived
and watched it fly inland.
When I'm old I would like to have saved something
to give you—the soft shreds
of a turquoise t-shirt we both claimed,
a jar of rain from a long Sunday afternoon
when we sat on the floor and listened
to sides of albums you'd never played,
the stub of a candle we lit in a mountain cabin
as the new year turned . . . —but why wait?
Metal fatigue;
the inexplicable virus;
a stray bullet in the police pursuit:
I need no reason and I have many.

A few days ago, I sat on a bench outside
the Episcopal Church in a small Indiana town
and waited for you. The July heat thickened shadows
and bent the necks of the daylilies;
I couldn't read the hour on the sundial.
And though I knew your gait,
the changing shape of your face
as you break into a smile,
your hands gesturing
as if they might suddenly toss me
a discus of the slippery light,
I held my breath
as though you were a stranger
who would change my life
walking into my life.

I want the sight of you, ankles stained green,
when you come in from cutting the grass,
the taste of you on my hands in the morning;
I will give you what I've hoarded
and, when I'm frightened into doubt, think
of the night I was afraid to climb
the ladder that led to a warehouse roof
and the city's best view
of the fireworks and how you were behind me all the way,
your hands on either side of my knees,
the sound of your voice,
Don't look down,
you can do it. And I did,
emerging shaken and breathless
into the night's splendid fake stars.

The Star's Etruscan Argument

I could be almost anywhere, beside the Atlantic
or in the desert, on a boat never designed to sail,
but I'm not, I'm in the hotel of a casino

on an Indian reservation in the deep south,
a sovereign nation in a county still unable
to resolve a murder forty years old. Four a.m.

& my mind's wheeling in huge ambits,
as if through an empty sky, the green numbers
on the digital clock ticking toward morning:

I turn on the television to the hotel channel,
where they teach you how to play roulette & blackjack,
then switch to an old movie I loved in college.

My window opens not to the world but on to the floor
& when I part the curtains the mild gold light
of the lamp is swallowed up by the casino's whiter,

cooler, cleaner light. Half past four & row after row
of people are playing slot machines; driven,
stoic, they don't pull the lever but instead punch

over & over a square lit button that places bets
faster & with less effort, all visceral pleasure,
the smooth glide of expensive equipment, removed.

If the window opened I'd hear the sound of waitresses
pushing drinks, the click of disposable lighters,
the muscular toll of coins hitting metal trays

& beneath all that a fabricated soundtrack of luck & fortune,
money singing, the bruit of machines hitting big.
Their eyes gleam with hope & its opposite,

which is also hope: the tinsel change of a small windfall;
free passes to the buffet, its bounty of crab legs
& fried shrimp, a chef carving thick slabs

of prime rib; or the big score, the million dollars
that would change their lives completely & forever.
These days memory is assembled from consumption's

debris, the promise of happiness or the crumpled containers
in which the promise was wrapped. How quickly
smoke swirling from a hundred cigarettes dissolves

above their heads: invisible systems at work, & God
not looking out for any of us from the inverted
domes in the ceiling that watch & record everything.

Aleda Shirley was born in Sumter, South Carolina, and, because her father was in the military, moved frequently as a child. She earned a B.A. in English from the University of Louisville in 1975 and in 1990 moved from Kentucky to Oklahoma. A few years later she moved to Mississippi, where she spent the rest of her life.

Shirley's books of poetry are *Chinese Architecture,* which won the Poetry Society of America's 1987 Norma Farber First Book Award, *Long Distance,* and *Dark Familiar.* She also published two chapbooks, *Rilke's Children* and *Silver Ending,* which won the Stanley Hanks Chapbook Competition of the St. Louis Poetry Society. Shirley received fellowships from the National Endowment for the Arts, the Kentucky Foundation for Women, the Mississippi Arts Commission, and the Kentucky Arts Council, and her poems appeared in such magazines as the *American Poetry Review, Kenyon Review, Poetry,* and *Virginia Quarterly Review.*

She was the first Poet in the Schools in a Kentucky program that became a national model through the National Endowment for the Arts. Shirley taught creative writing to young students in the Jefferson County (Mississippi) Public School system and became a Millsaps College writer-in-residence, inspiring students at both Millsaps and the University of Mississippi.

Shirley's book *Long Distance* was written in the years after she moved from Oklahoma to Mississippi, and reflects, she said, the upheavals she felt during that time in her life. Her last book, *Dark Familiar,* garnered praise from critics throughout the country. One critic, Lucie Brock-Broido, wrote: "Aleda Shirley is a feline writer, stealthy and carnal and lush. In *Dark Familiar* she has staked her claims, the familiar, deeply human ones: that emptiness is permanent, that hope is tenuous, that connection is infinite, but that the body is exact in danger, prone to bad luck and to miracle—and all within that brutal, brave phenomenon where one is settling the debt of one's terrestrial accounts. These narratives are harrowing, and hallowed, striking, dark, familiar, strange, and beautiful, and wise."

In an interview that accompanied reviewers' copies of *Dark Familiar,* Shirley said that the book "is, in many ways, a dialogue with death, and the elegies in the book are both elegies for specific people, but also, I hope, something more than that: an attempt to preserve times that would otherwise be lost forever and the taking of a stance of strength in the face of grief and loss."

She died June 16, 2008, after a long battle with cancer.

SARAH
Gorham

b. 1956

Sickle Billed Hummingbird

You think at first of a fated
mishap: trying to free himself
from a notch in the wood, the bird
buzzed frantically, bent
and nearly split in two his long,
thread-like bill. But no, the curve's
a fine tuned connection—homage
paid to a blossom's hooked corolla,
its nectar hidden deep within apricot-
colored petals.

Famished every three minutes,
darting from pistil to pistil, the pollen
on his back, he's an utter slave.
And the plant, aged aristocrat,
would perish without his attention.
Sometimes desire so matches its object,
it's like the two once lived as one:
man and woman, breast and mouth,
kindling and fire. This match is so right

flower is touched by sickle billed
hummingbird alone and the bird, in turn,
has let down his guard
shedding his cocky plumage
for a robe of lusterless brown.
No other species dares interrupt
their conversation held lip to lip.
Only at night do they part,
plunge into a metabolic torpor,

conceding with their souls
that heat and light peel away
with the slightest wind
and a kiss, however perfect,
is held for only so long.

Late Evening Love Poem

Don't ask me to stop the dark
slipping into this poem.
I met you in the dark (lines one and three!)
under a Norway pine. Night country.
Lost my flashlight. Pitch
stuck to my bare feet and thighs.
So sure I'd marry a blonde,
but your hair was black.
In Fiji it's a sin to touch a person's hair
but make him a lover
and the taboo disappears.
When kissing we shut our eyes—
inside it's deep mahogany,
licorice, black coffee. Delicious. I was
floating blind
in a year-long gloom.
You were a star in the lit world
and then you fell, a dark
to benefit your poems.
The saying goes, "A man
too good for the world
is no good for his wife." (Yiddish)
We need the dark for seeing inside.
I crashed into you and stars
punctuated my eyelids.
The experts call them "phosphenes."
Scarlet fever will bring them on.
And delirium tremors. Some think
they're explanation for a saint's
visions. Love's door is hinged

with pain. My mother died;
her dying guided me
to you. My favorite sound
is insects in the dark,
rubbing their thighs together. Your jeans
and black silk jacket and shiny
buckled belt. Black makes me thin
and you, hip. How I love
the forties hat that shades your eyes.
I lost my flashlight and bumped into you.
It was an accident. Lucky accident.
Lucky dark.

Honeymoon, Pleasant Hill

Poor sinners, we wandered too far,
lured by those trim Shaker fences
like lace on the good mother's slip.

We slumped in chairs meant to straighten the spine.
Ran our fingers over testicle-shaped finials,
our palms down the Trustees' railing,

smooth as a woman's thigh.
Damn that was good pie, we exclaimed
to the waiter in his Shaker smock.

He cracked a smile (only three survive
in upstate Maine), and kept that
Shaker food coming. Baby

corn, vegetables soaked in lemon oil,
mashed potatoes swollen
around our steak. We tossed and turned the night,

our Shaker beds sheeted too tight—
and woke to labor that zig-zag dance.
First a hum from inside out, then the verse

pitched from brother east to sister west,
against the boards faster, the telltale
thump, heels dug in for good purchase.

Finally, the dousing with an ecstatic shout.
(So sure the Shakers were their Godly Version
would bear the future out.)

I Go Back

Back into longing and expectation
and my body again plumps up.
I had worn it with indifference.

I go back into grief, to the beached
dolphin I touched
with just two fingers,

to the shoestring, radio antenna,
fishing line I left hanging.
Hope finally meets its little fish,

finds it smaller than expected.
I go back into sunsuits, terrycloth,
my skin fiery underneath,

back when the wanting was richer
than anything I own,
when my wrist bones floated

and my skull was unlocked.
When pinpricks on the horizon
blossomed into sailboats

and I memorized their names.
Yes, I go back into longing,
attention, to precision,

with my vagueness and my years
and my sarcasm like water
rushing into a hole in the sand.

President and editor in chief of Sarabande Books in Louisville, **Sarah Gorham** was born in Santa Monica, California, and raised in a literary household. Her early interest in literature, however, did not lead her on a direct path to her current position as head of an independent literary press. She worked as a firefighter, a sports-information director for a women's basketball team, an assistant to the poetry advisor at the Folger Shakespeare Library, a newsletter editor for CityTrust Bank, an alternative high school teacher, and an artist in residence with the Kentucky Arts Council before cofounding Sarabande Books in 1994.

Gorham, who holds an M.F.A. from the University of Iowa, has published three books of poetry—*The Cure, The Tension Zone,* and *Don't Go Back to Sleep*—and coedited, with Jeffrey Skinner, an anthology titled *Last Call: Poems on Alcoholism, Addiction, and Deliverance.* Her poems have been published in the country's most prestigious literary magazines, including *American Poetry Review, Antaeus,* the *Georgia Review,* the *Paris Review,* the *Kenyon Review,* the *Nation,* and *Poetry.*

Her numerous honors and awards include an Al Smith Fellowship from the Kentucky Arts Council, a Writer's Choice Award from *Prairie Schooner,* the Carolyn Kizer Award from *Poetry Northwest,* and inclusion in *2006 Best American Poetry,* selected by Billy Collins. She has held fellowships at Yaddo, the MacDowell Colony, the Wurlitzer Foundation, and the Virginia Center for the Creative Arts. Gorham has also served as a judge and panelist for the National Endowment for the Arts, the Illinois Arts Council, and the New Hampshire Arts Council.

The poetry she most admires, Gorham says, includes Renaissance poetry and the work of W. S. Merwin, Louise Glück, Elizabeth Bishop, and Louise Bogan. "Now I love the Eastern European poets because they access the dream world far better than we do."

She is married to the poet Jeffrey Skinner.

TONY
Crunk

b. 1956

Visiting the Site of One of the First Churches
My Grandfather Pastored

My mother said later that, to the shovel operators, we must have
looked like some delegation from out of town that couldn't find the
picnic. Or else the funeral. Not so bad my brother and me jumping
the fence, and my father, but then my mother, and all of us helping
my grandfather over, and finally my grandmother deciding she
wanted to see, too.

Then all of us standing together at the rim of the pit in our Sunday
clothes, sun reflecting off my grandmother's black patent purse, a
few trees still hanging on nearby, roots exposed, like tentacles, like
the earth is shrinking under them. The smell of sulphur.

The giant bucket scoops up through the rocks and dirt, the shovel
swings around, the bucket empties, and the whole thing swings
back, the noise taking an extra second to reach us. I am watching the
two men inside, expecting them to notice us, to wave us away
because we don't belong there, but they don't. They must be used
to it.

Years later I will remember my grandfather saying that they strip
away the land but all they put back is the dirt. Maybe plant a few
scrub pine. "Good for nothing any more," he says now, turning to
go back to the car. "Good for nothing except holding the rest of
the world together."

It looks almost blue in the sun, the piece of coal I have picked up
to take home for a souvenir.

Souvenirs

for my father

Through the mirror
I can see you reading
your new testament before bed,
putting it away in the dresser drawer
where you keep

the tin box of foreign coins
and the hand-tinted postcards
of Italy
you brought home from the Navy
in 1954.

We lie awake
my brother and I
listening to you on the back steps
singing
only half to yourself
a snatch of an old miner's song
that goes:

up every day
in the dawn's early light

to go down in a hole
where it's already night

it's already night
boys it's already night,

and through the window
I watch the fireflies
among the trees,
which,
you told us once,
were dead people lighting cigarettes.

Elders

1.

My father remembers
fire: blown sparks
from his Uncle Buell's smithing iron
scorching red
eyes in the lilac leaves;
transparent scarves of yellow flame
smoking up from the locust boles
into a lowering February
sky—him and his father

burning off a new tobacco bed;
him and his grandfather
hunting
camped on a bluff above the Cumberland
the two of them
sitting under scattershot stars
his grandfather telling him
of seeing, as a boy,

The City of Clifton
blow its boiler
off the Birmingham landing,
my father dreaming
that night
of hearing the stricken
cries of the perishing,
of seeing that fire
out on the water . . .

2.

My father remembers
a needlepoint picture:
Jesus seated in Glory
with the words

Christ is the Head
       Of This House
The Unseen Guest
       At Every Meal
The Silent Listener
       To Every Conversation

that hung above his father's
kitchen chair,
who'd lean back after Sunday dinner
and sing out,

"Well I'm most done traveling
this rough rocky road
and it's time my soul headed home"—
a game he had with the kids

—who'd sing out,
"Papa
what will you do
if you can't afford the hearse?"

"Sit on my bed
and wait for angels to come."

"What will you do
if you can't afford the preacher?"

"Pay him with quarters
I stole from the moon."

"Papa, what will you do
if you can't afford the casket?"

"Charge it to the wind," he'd sing,
"and let the dust settle it . . ."

3.
My father remembers lying awake
listening to the locusts in the orchard

chirring to split their skins
listening for the screech owl

haunting the cedars' attic rooms
and finally the Jackson Flyer

blue traveler
taking the high curve out of Orton Station

unwinding her long black veil across the Barrens
moaning it out by midnight—

once for those she takes away
twice for those she's leaving.

After Visiting Home for Christmas

A few rows in front of me on the bus, two boys, maybe ten or
eleven, are waving at cars that pass us on the Interstate, trying to get
people to wave back, falling into their seat to laugh about it. They're
with the group of deaf kids that gets on in Louisville on Sundays, on
their way back to the State School in Danville. The sky is thickening
with twilight and low clouds, a few flakes.

Just beyond Midway a car passes, the boys wave, and the car slows
down, staying even with the bus. The woman on the passenger side
is gesturing to the boys, they're gesturing back—it takes me a second
to realize they are talking to each other. Three or four of the other
kids come around to watch.

They talk that way for several miles. Then the woman waves good-
bye, and the boys wave, it getting too dark by then for them
to see . . .

A native of Hopkinsville, Kentucky, **Tony Crunk** has published two chapbooks of poetry, *Parables and Revelations* and *Cumberland;* a collection of short fiction, *Stories from Real Life;* three children's books; and a book-length collection of poems, *Living in the Resurrection,* which was selected by Mary Oliver as the winner of the Yale Series of Younger Poets award in 1994. His poems have appeared in many prestigious magazines and journals, including the *Georgia Review, Virginia Quarterly Review, Paris Review,* and *Poetry Northwest.* He is currently a professor of English at the University of Alabama at Birmingham.

Crunk says growing up in Hopkinsville had everything to do with his becoming a poet. "Growing up there, I felt it was a very limited and limiting place on the one hand but, later, came to cherish deeply the cultural, social, religious inheritance I received from Hopkinsville and its people. My need to sort through those ambivalent feelings and make peace with them is what led me to begin writing seriously in my late twenties."

Specifically, it was a serendipitous "meeting" with Zbigniew Herbert that led him to begin writing poetry. "I was walking through the University of Virginia library and saw an anthology of post-war Polish poetry on a filing cart. I opened the book randomly to Herbert's 'Study of the Object,' and was smitten into slobbering amazement. Starting there, I went on to soak up as much modern and contemporary Eastern European poetry as I could." He lists Lucille Clifton, Charles Simic, Charles Wright, and Gregory Orr as other important poetic influences.

On "Elders": "This poem is from a longer work that addresses the forced relocation, from the mid-1930s through mid-1960s, of some 22,000 people from western Kentucky and Tennessee to make way for Kentucky Lake, Lake Barkley, and Land Between the Lakes National Recreation Area. Writing about this project, I felt I was extending the scope of my inquiry from my more personal early poems into why and how I became the person I have become. Although my family was not directly affected by the relocation, this historical experience seemed emblematic of the dislocation, and its losses, that transpired between my parents' generation and my own in many places in small-town America. I think lots of folks my age are haunted, and shaped, by that loss of a place and its culture that they did not know and cannot return to."

NIKKY
Finney

b. 1957

Sex

After being told, "Oh what would you know
about it anyway."

How the room rained down
a mother's only blistering ash,
her words lifting then settling
clear and hot, then the branding
of me complete.

After she proclaimed
to the rest of the family
that whatever it is I do
with another woman
could never even-steven
to what she does with daddy.

As if my way to human pleasure
too inefficient to be called the same.
As if we who do with a woman
should find a new name
for the doing.

She, believing that my body
coming together with another
woman's a fake freak of nature,
not sex or love and could never be.

The sermon of her looks
always the same.

How my pot of woman
is not worth its salt

because there is not the pepper
of a man there.
That, in order for any woman
to cook up a thing worth
sensually serving
a lid and seasoning
of a certain fit and taste
is required.

That what I offer to the diamond
and life of another woman, that
then streams up my two front
female spines, that branches off
into a desert orchid, that grows
into a family of complicated
spiraly things in the middle
of any hot springs geyser night,
is not worth its weight in sweat.

As if what I know about pleasure
and the microscopic fittings of love,
about the filling of an appetite
that lives somewhere between
my cerebellum and my thigh tissue,
that runs like a southern railroad
trestle to my heart bone emptying
next into my lung sacs, as if that
tenderness which douses all the gates
of my body clean and wet like all
the steamed water and wind that
ever was in the world suddenly
let loose, as if what comes from

the zest and tongue of another
woman's capsule to my own;
that intricate complicated vessel
of how and what we shape our
loving into, cannot be compared
to what she has felt between her
own gulf stream.

Mama, what appears shut sky
to you, is heaven opened wide
to me.

Black Orion

The Star Man Was Frederick J. Davenport
(1903–1992)

In his orbiting eyes we are all slaves   still
and there are more new ones of us born everyday
slavish to things we can not do without
slavish to whatever is new and fandangled
polished and pearled

In his cornfield while waiting for grouse to stir
to shoot and freeze for christmas he told me
I am leaving a world of slaves behind   Girl
so what am I really leaving
time to go   when that's all what's left
each of you are every letter of the wanting rainbow
no wonder you define loneliness by what you do not have
There at least   I'll be around things that ain't so beholdin'

A star man has lifted off the ground
A brilliant man is walking weightless through his clouds

A man who did not know that things had ever changed
because he beheld the sky as something that may shift
but was forever dependably exact
A man who did not believe that things *should* ever change
his only concern was up
his channel was the shifting sky and the always ground
he found scripture in the tissue thin pages of the almanac
A man who did not want to know the answer to it all
who liked it the old way just fine

In college astronomy   1959
Fred J. Davenport wrote a paper
he predicted that in ten years   more or less
a man would walk the moon
and would he be a slave too
of course he would
if he turned around and came back here

Handing in these dreamy notions
to learned men who graded him poorly
Slaves he said of them all
as he sat before their limited eyes

Slaves would only see it as luminated soil
the star man saw it as real and therefore   walkable
his prediction missed by only weeks

This blazing unfettered man
who spent his life staring at the sky
more than he kept up or eye on any human spheres
knew   he scared me how he   knew
Don't get on the road until Lyra lines up with Orion
Yes Sir   He knew

Barley colored
bespeckled
tincaps and goobers always in his pockets
cracked shells   his human droppings all over his land
The real money

At night he would stand before the sky
arms folded and alone
a motionless dragon nostrilling the dark
breaking bread at his terrestrial table
and tossing Dr. Carver seeds as he came and went
preaching always about the arrangement of above
and nothing else
his white cornsilk hair moving downwind
like a cloud of gas and dust

The Black Orion
who planted taters and melons
by the aggregates of lights and darks
by shooting stars and the aurora australis
explained I was a slave
because I could never stay long enough
to see his meteors' shower
because I could never come and visit him alone
there in his pinetree galaxy
teeming with red dust bowls and candleflies
and to his unbuttoned eyes
There   it was always too sacred and dark
too perfect and complete
to ever welcome any hardbound no count book

So many times I came up his road
a skinny empty handed woman
and left a fat imaginative girl
with too many presents for my arms to carry

It is sunday and in calling   home
I hear Mama say   He's gone
the star man left the ground today
lifted off without me
just like he said he would
gone up
away far
far from all us clinging sightless slaves

The New Cotton

They are just boys, chain
ganged to the side of the road,
dressed to the nines in sunny
orange, that shade of red that
never seems to set, familiar
color of that foreign flower,
the kind you can close your
eyes in sleep and still see, but
these boys are not flowers
anymore, no
thing that can be seen to bloom
has been left to bloom, in this
place where a chain around a
Black man's ankle is the state
jewel, but if you still own your
eyes you know they are still boys.

They do not yet know how to
bend, someone has not yet
passed on the secret
of how to save their backs
for the rest of the journey,
someone forgot to offer the
old way of how to get through
the whip of their young days
in order to reach the sweet
rock of their old, they angle
and arc carelessly, not knowing
they are match
sticks of American history,

never squatting down low
in the grass, never bending
at the ankle or thigh, they are
such proud brittle lion trees
about to break in every
direction but free, the weave
of all their fabric wasted
in the constant picking up
of useless plastic things,
that as I get closer,
that as I pass,
look white and sticky plump,
some kind of new cotton
stuck inside their reaching
Robeson hands.

The Making of Paper

for Toni Cade Bambara (1939–1995)

In the early '80s, I spent two years in a writing workshop that Toni Cade Bambara held in her Atlanta home. Anybody in the community who was writing was welcome. I adored the opportunity to sit at this great writer's feet who knew so much about so much. In 1990, she moved to Philadelphia and was later diagnosed with cancer. We talked on the long-distance line when we could. I would always ask if there was anything she needed that I could send. She usually answered no. But in our last conversation, which took place one week before she crossed over, she held the phone a little longer. "Maybe," she said, "maybe you could send some paper and what about one of those fat juicy pens?"

Imagine that,
you asking me for paper.

For the record let me state
I would hunt a tree down for you,
stalk it until it fell
all loud and out of breath
in the forest.

Much as I love a tree,
fat, tall and free.

As anti-violent and pro-vegetarian
as I am.
Never been much
for strapping a gun
to any of my many hips,
for any reason whatsoever,
but on the copper penny eyes

of my grandmother, I tell you
this: I would hunt a tree down for you.

And when found
I would pull it all the way down the road
through congested city streets all by myself
and deliver it straight away
to your hospital bed,
one single extra-large floral arrangement,
something loud and free,
with red and purple bow.

Or better yet,
this tree loving
gun hating Geechee girl
would strap a wild west
gun belt machete
around her hips
enter the worst part of the woods alone
and go trunk to trunk
until the right one appeared
growing peaceful in its thousand-year-old
natal pot.

Look it
right in its
round rough ancient eyes
and confess away,
tell it straight to its woody face,
my about to do deed.

I'd even touch it
on its limbs,
fingers begging forgiveness,
give as much comfort to it
as I could, while trying to
explain the necessaryness
of its impending death;
me standing there,
my *Gorilla My Love* eyes
spilling all over everything,
sending up papyrus prayers
that all begin with,
"I'm so sorry but Toni Cade needs paper."

Only then would I slash its lovely body
into one million thin black cotton rag sheets
just your uncompromising size.

Send you some paper?
Oh yes,
paper is coming Toni Cade
wagonloads
in the name
of your sweet Black writing life,
from Black writers everywhere
refusing to leave
the arena
to the fools.

Paper is on the way.

A professor of English at the University of Kentucky, **Nikky Finney** has published four books—*The World Is Round, Heartwood, Rice,* and *On Wings Made of Gauze*—and edited an anthology titled *The Ringing Ear: 100 Contemporary African American Poets Write About the American South.* The recipient of several grants and awards, including the Provost's Distinguished Professor Award at the University of Kentucky, a Pen American Book Award, and an Al Smith Fellowship from the Kentucky Arts Council, Finney has published in numerous magazines, journals, and anthologies.

A founding member of the Affrilachian Poets, a group of black writers with strong ties to Appalachia, she has read her poetry and fiction at dozens of universities in the United States, including the University of Alabama, University of Pittsburgh, Yale University, Smith College, Duke University, and Oberlin College, and has taught workshops and given public lectures at the Gwendolyn Brooks Writer's Conference, the International Black Women's Film Festival, the National Black Women's Health Project, and the Africa World Arts Festival.

Born less than a half mile from the Atlantic Ocean in Conway, South Carolina, Finney says she has felt an affinity for saltwater since she was a young girl. "The sound and the feel of the ocean are always in my head and heart. I sought out its shore and waters as a girl and found there the birthplace of my imagination, my curiosity."

The first poets she came to know as a child were Gwendolyn Brooks, Langston Hughes, Emily Dickinson, Robert Frost, and Walt Whitman, and in her teenage years became attracted to the poets of the Black Arts Movement: Mari Evans, Nikki Giovanni, Sonia Sanchez, and Carolyn Rodgers. She adds, "I very much admire the work of Lucille Clifton—her unadorned, sizzling images and heartfelt stories."

On "Black Orion": "This poem is about my grandfather's brother, Fred J. Davenport, a farmer who was always a little offbeat and talked about religion, science, literature, and geology. At night, he would stand out in his fields staring at the dark, silvery sky. He was a quiet man who could grow anything in the dark, red dirt. He taught me to love words and their definitions. He taught me to seek out my own truths. He predicted a man would walk on the moon ten years before one did. How did he know this? (It wasn't until graduate school that I learned African people had been reading the sky for millions of years.) He taught me to love the earth, taught me that inanimate things have heartbeats."

DON
Boes

b. 1958

Feature Race

Over the last furlong the favorite faltered.

From the rail I stared at the blinkered horse,
its pink and blue silks flapping in the sun—

the Venezuelan jockey, low in the saddle,

whipping as if he meant to scar forever

the expensive and sweating thoroughbred.
I lost my money on that now-forgotten animal

though for one minute and 42 seconds

I flirted with winning and its responsibility.

The replay revealed the drama of the final charge:
even the long shots, wearied by the weight

of our petty cash, crowded into a chorus of speed.

Paving Kentucky

Limestone or shale or sandstone,
it makes no difference;

we can safely engineer
any physiography.

We can chisel a cloverleaf
out of a misplaced mountain

or scrape a valley
of all natural inconveniences

so light bulbs and bourbon
can coast toward shiny

airports & malls.

Distracted mares
foal

in the shadows
of grander openings.

Demolished hills
give us no reason to stop.

Reunion

for E. L.

The cleanliness of alphabetical order

> escapes us.

My eighth-grade sweetheart

> is already absent,

dead for seven years

> and me no wiser until now,

my assignments shuffled,

> her spot in the line lost.

No bullet or highway accident

> turned the trick

but rather

> a poorly engineered blood vessel

shipped her back

> as far as she could go, resoftened.

That's all I comprehend

> though her best friend

offers me details of doctors

> and their durable charm.

A class roster for a guide,

> I look into faces

the way I squinted

> at the shiny blackboard

before my sight, faulty but not fatal,

> was fixed.

Like siblings

> summoned to an emergency homecoming

we mingle at top speed,

> our reminiscing

a rainless thunder

> that steeps the parish hall.

A few of us brazen celebrants,
                        with a vitality
undelayed since graduation,
                        rise from bingo tables
to float loosely
            in the moonlight of our first playgound.
A candle sputtering past midnight,
                        my grief grows ragged.
More than once,
                in college town or apartment complex,
I thought she numbered among the crowd
                        but now
she's a prompt, a splinter I can't dig out.
                        In the linkage
of the present
            and what used to be the present
I remember recess
            and how we seldom spoke,
the weeping willow
                in her parents' yard,
the wire fence,
            the slack knots of honeysuckle,
her on one side,
            me on the other.

For Charles Mingus (1922–1979)

In the last days you continued to create.
From a wheelchair you weaved the mathematic
of your final compositions, a bass line
that maneuvered across the sparse
backdrop of pain.   Tonight I listen

to what you made: ballads, blues,
anthems of church-jazz, parables and portraits
of the sonic world.   Around me
the rest of the world rattles with the poverty

of time.   The rest of the world is noise.

Born in Louisville, **Don Boes** has published a chapbook, *Railroad Crossing*, and a book-length collection of poetry, *The Eighth Continent*, which was chosen by A. R. Ammons for the Samuel Morse Poetry Prize in 1993. A professor of English at Bluegrass Community and Technical College, Boes has published poems in *Indiana Review, Seattle Review, Prairie Schooner,* the *Louisville Review, Crazyhorse,* and others. He has held residencies at the MacDowell Colony in New Hampshire and the Ragdale Foundation, and has received three Al Smith Fellowships from the Kentucky Arts Council.

He says his list of mentors "is extensive and continues to grow." During his undergraduate days at Centre College in Danville, Kentucky, he took workshops with Carolyn Kizer and Ruth Whitman. At Indiana University, where he earned an M.F.A. in poetry in 1985, he studied with Philip Appleman, Maura Stanton, and Roger Mitchell. "Roger was an especially important influence," Boes states. "Like all good workshop leaders and poets, Roger is many things—wise and judicious, eccentric and wryly humorous." Among other contemporary poets Boes lists as influential are Charles Wright, Linda Gregg, and Dean Young. "I admire these poets because they have remained true to their own poetic sensibilities while at the same time exploring subjects large and small. In my own way, I try to pay attention to these same two concerns in every poem I write: art and communication."

On "For Charles Mingus": "'Me, Myself an Eye' was one of the first jazz records in my collection. Even though the album was released under his name, Charles Mingus was extremely ill with ALS at the time of these recordings, so did not play his customary bass at any of the sessions. Instead, he was the leader and composer and visionary of the musical venture. My poem 'For Charles Mingus' is an appreciation of the man and his spirit."

KATHLEEN
Driskell

b. 1959

Optometrist's Visit

Sitting in the driveway,
noticing in a strange way and looming,
but certainly focused way, the finials
of the fenceposts, the eaves

where the dark paint curled
like burning paper, a blue martin
fading against the winter sky,

she thought maybe it was because
she had loved him too well for so long

that when the bright lights
went off in that narrow office and
the handsome new optometrist's
smooth palms cupped her face,

guided her face toward the stereoscope
and he prompted close and raspy *how's
that, now this, dear,
now is this better?*
she realized

it had been years since
in the dark she had been touched by
another man and at once the world
came again quick and dangerous and
she still felt her face
held in those warm hands,
her knees pressed tight

against his and she thought
even without her new glasses,
it was now senseless to think, given
this new possibility, that a soft blur
could ever truly exist anywhere again

and it was with a sorrowful reluctance
that she rolled up her window,

got out, locked her door
and walked up the steps
of what, for so long, she had called
their home.

Why I Mother You the Way I Do

That afternoon, I have to admit, there were no thoughts
of you. I was in high school, making my way past
the buses to a waiting car—a boy who would not be
your father—when the line of traffic stopped. The girls,
classmates, sisters, had darted between buses
and into the highway, trying to cross the field to their home.
They both lay twisted in the road. My science teacher,
Mr. Desaro, took off his suit coat and laid it over Susan's
face. He was crying because he only had one coat.

By the time they let us pass, Eve had been covered with a white
sheet. The ambulances had come. Red lights flashed, but
their mother was still pushing her silver cart
through the grocery. The sheriff was walking up behind
her. As she reached for a gallon of milk, he moved
to touch her arm.

With a Shiner, My Husband
Enters the Flower Shop

I should be thinking about him and how
he could have lost an eye when
the malignant scaffolding collapsed and a 2

× 4 dropped through the air on the job
site the morning of our nineteenth anniversary, but
I'm considering her, the florist

looking up from her table to see
him walking in sheepish, head-
bowed, ringing the bell as he enters.

I'm wondering how many times
she's arranged roses for the wounded,
the bruised, the stitched hungry male

who needs her help—*and fast.*
And I wonder if she imagines me,
black cast iron skillet,

cocked in hand like a baseball bat
as she pulls out the three stems
of delphinium, blue as a bruised

heart and two full hydrangea,
pink petaled and soft as boxed
lingerie. There is not baby's breath,

I'm relieved to see, nor
the red lips of soft roses,
nor the ubiquitous and overly cheerful

mum. She knows, somehow, what
he does not—preoccupied with his day
to day—that even a good long marriage holds

small hurts that barb and fester
near the skin, so she reaches
for the balm of calm sweep

of palm leaf, that healer of the unsaid
argument of morning, the rising blood
as I watched him back out

in his truck, his having forgotten—once
again—this morning of all mornings—
to hang up the towel, curled

like a wet dog asleep on the bathroom
floor. A long marriage remembers
its youth as a roan, muscled horse, rearing,

with nostrils flaring.

                    I accept this
bouquet for what I could have said
but didn't, and hold onto the thin

healing. I accept too, finally, that often
a long marriage is a donkey schlepping
across the desert. Tender-eyed, I attempt

to once again re-love husband as self,
to heal the wounded eye as one tries
to heal self. And accept the vase

on the table which stands to remind,
each day as I change its water,
that even this good marriage

is from time to time a sorry animal, in need,
and over burdened, but grateful for the hard
day it's about to close sore eyes against.

To the Outdoor Wedding

All come, forgive, and bless the dogmatic over-ripe bride
who insists she will be married in the garden

of her dead mother, though the guests and wedding party
hiss and shiver as the light rain turns unrepentantly

to pelting ice. All rise, and love the narrow bridesmaids,
numb and under-dressed in lavender slivers of spaghetti strap,

and listen to their teeth chatter as they scurry down
the aisle, drawn to the collective body heat

of the groomsmen and minister shifting from foot
to foot under the wavering trellis of altar. Praise

the wind picking up mightily, and the groom, unsteady
and sallow, who does not beam when she appears

in blown splendor on her father's arm—and the guests
who are wet-faced, their heads bowed down

to keep the sleet from stinging. It is the bride, prayer-
ful and confident in her white faith, we have to thank

when a gust picks up and wraps her long veil three times
around her father's head, shrouding him from the booming

garden tent about to unpluck itself from the soggy ground.
Who else but her to be thankful to when instead of the tent,

her veil snaps free from the father's flailing and lifts high,
then thrashes away over the Indiana cornfields, just now

brilliant in their new spring greening—the green shine,
the sumptuous periwinkle sky, the brilliant white strata

folding into itself, and dropping its knot—but wait! Again
the wind sends it sailing and the guests, heads up now,

mouths open in a collected prayer of *ah* and *ah* as the veil
transforms into a bucking Chinese dragon, taking away

all that is old, folding, dancing off and far. The guests
gather themselves and offer the warm utterance

ooh when from the thawing and newly planted fields
a thousand black starlings lift in alarm.

Kathleen Driskell teaches creative writing, serves as associate program director of the M.F.A. in Writing Program at Spalding University in Louisville, and is the associate editor of the *Louisville Review*. She has published two books of poetry—*Laughing Sickness* and *Seed Across Snow*—as well as poems in *River Styx*, *North American Review*, the *Southern Review*, and *New Millennium Writings*.

The recipient of an Al Smith Fellowship from the Kentucky Arts Council and winner of the Henry Leadingham Poetry Prize from the Frankfort Arts Foundation, Driskell says she came to poetry through narrative, specifically stories told by her mother, grandmother, and aunts at her grandmother's house in Indianapolis. "Nearly every weekend, we'd drive from Louisville to my grandmother's home, and while the men were in the den watching sports on TV, the women would continue the ritual of sifting through a big cardboard box heaped with loose photographs. Each photograph was the impulse for some crazy or winsome story. Always, it was about reaching back. Thinking about those times, it's really not that much of a surprise that I became a poet. My own poems usually begin first with an image and then go about linking those 'pictures' to narrative."

Driskell says her earliest literary influence was Emily Dickinson, whose work made Driskell understand that form and content are linked in great poetry. She grew to learn about and love poetic technique, she says, through the American Modernists: Frost, Moore, Williams, and Stevens.

On "Why I Mother You the Way I Do": "When I was a high school junior, two of my classmates were hit by a car in front of our school just following the afternoon dismissal. As the deputy directed our long string of cars past the accident scene, we drove by. I've never been able to exorcise the image of the girls covered with white sheets in the road. The poem itself centers on my realization that my children are parented by my past and that many of my mothering decisions come from considering the before and after of a life-changing and often sorrowful event. In this poem's case, the life before the mother is informed of her daughters' deaths and the life after. I'm talking about the greatest fear a mother has always at the back of her mind—that of losing her child."

FRANK X
Walker

b. 1962

God's House

*The expedition left the Louisville, Kentucky, area
near the Falls of the Ohio on October 26, 1803.*

When we first left Kentucke
the trees had commenced to dressing up
the fall harvest an the garden
was already full a pumpkins an squash.

Massa Clark didn't ask me to go on no expedition.
He just say "pack" an pointed to the door.
So I gather up what little I got an more than I can carry a his
an head off to a sail-bearing keelboat
where his friend Massa Lewis is waiting.
That boat was so big
you could lay any ten a the sixteen men on board
or eight a me head to toe an still have enough
room for the dog.

We start out on the Ohio an swing up the old man a rivers.
When we gets to the mouth a the dark woman
they calls the Big Muddy
we sets up winter camp a good canoe ride from Saint Louie.

That spring when the rains come we cross the Mississippi
an commence to climbing the M'soura
an float right up through heaven on earth
more sky than I ever seen, rocks as pretty as trees
an game so plentiful they come right down to the river bank
an invites they selves to dinner.

Now, I ain't what you would call
a scripture quoter, but the first time
I seen the water fall at M'soura,
felt a herd a buffalo stampede
an looked down from top
a Rock Mountains, it was like church.

An where else but God's house can a body servant
big as me, carry a rifle, hatchet ana bone handle knife
so sharp it can peel the black off a lump a coal
an the white man
still close his eyes an feel safe, at night?

Promises

It does not require many words to speak the truth.
—Chief Joseph, Nez Perce

Many tribes speak they piece
by talking with they hands an faces.
When we sit in the circle to talk
with Sacagawea's brother, the chief
she take his words in Shoshoni
an measure them out in Hidatsa
Charbono hands it to Lebiche in French
Lebiche gives it to the Captains in English
then they talks between themselves
an sends it back down the line
an so forth an so on.

The words seem to be on they own expedition
but it hard to believe the truth
can be traded on that many tongues
an still taste like itself.

Revisionist History

fired three rounds as we approached the shore and
landed oppocit the center of the Town, the people
gathered on the shore . . .
—William Clark, September 23, 1806

When we set foot back in old Saint Louie
there was much celebration an putting on
as everyone had give us up for dead.
We paraded through the streets firing our guns
an made a home in the nearest tavern.
No one seemed to tire a hearing us tell
our stories night after night.

After too many cups an tellers
there came tales a herds a grizzlies,
big talking fish an Indian women ten foot tall.

The truth seemed to stretch so
that by an by I seem to disappear from they tongues
as if I had never even been there
as if my blackness never saved they hides.

Them twist the tales an leave out my parts in it
so much so, that directly I become Massa Clark's boy, again
just along to cook
an carry.

Praise Song

York's hunting shirt

York be the strongest, blackest man
anybody this side of the big river has ever seen.
He might show his strength, strut, dance a jig,
or even tease the Indian children,

but he never brag 'bout that what make him
even more proud, that what connect him
to his true man-self, what the natives respect
him most for, his prowess and feats as a hunter.

What other slave you know carry a gun and a hatchet
and a knife sharp enough to split a man's ribs and still
his heart, but be too self mastered to even think on it?
Useful tools, knives and guns, but ain't no magic in them.

The magic was in York. He had the power.
How else you figure a man, twice as big as some,
larger than most, step in among the dead leaves
and wild things and simply disappear?

How else you think he walk right up on wild game
have it sniff the air, tweak its ears
and still not see him less than a touch away?
Standing as still as an oak. Breathing like the forest.

How you reckon he never bring home anything tough
and hard to chew, muscles still in shock from fear
or struggle? He took his game with so much speed
and skill the animals thought they was still alive.

Wrapped around him like a second skin, I hugged him
back into his true self, merged my scent with his,
transformed one of the ancestor's fiercest gifts—reduced
to a white man's slave—back into a real man again.

I swallowed his sweat when he fought with the great
grizzly bear. I felt his heart slow down as he walked
among herds of buffalo. He and I engaged in the dance
of hunting before his blade made the kill.

Like all before me, my two-tone skin is rich and thick
with the color of tree bark and makes him
one with the earth and bush whether the leaves be
on the ground or in the air.

The smell of the outdoors is ground deep into me:
perfume of grasshopper juice, huckleberries, bitter grasses,
animal dung, and the richness of fresh-turned dirt.
I would not be welcome at the fancy dinner table.

There are pouches of dried roots, coyote anklebones,
buffalo teeth, bear claws, and bird quills piercing
every part of me. I could ride his back for a hundred years
and you still could not tell us from the forest.

My purpose is simple. Protect him from harm, guarantee
he never go hungry, and connect him to the hunters, griots,
and sorcerers coursing through his veins. So I do just that
and raise his name in song.

Beacon

for Stephen Bishop, first guide & explorer of
Mammoth Cave, died June 15, 1859, in his 37th year

There was a time when adventurers
and curiosity seekers
from all over the world
rode for days by stagecoach and saddle
to follow a mysterious man
deep into the pitch black

Tall, dark, incandescent
slinging flaming cloth torches
into the distance
mood lighting
to show off the earth's inner beauty

His shadow and directions
bounced off wet, jagged ceilings and walls
His laughter echoed
and filled the cavernous corners
a warm beacon
as easy to follow as the hand-held
lard oil lamps

Today he lies in state
beneath a borrowed tombstone
above the historic entrance
of this deep hollow ground
a mammoth cave as familiar to him

as the inside of his own mouth
with miles of trails as recognizable as

the underground river of veins
on the back of his hands

They traveled to see a trailblazer
They came to follow a dark man
with the power to shine light
on our unspoken subterranean fears

What better tool for abolition's sake
than a slave
leading the way into the depths
and out of our collective darkness

Last Words

words and hugs
were not my daddy's tools
life was about work
hands were made to think

he communicated like his father
silently erecting monuments of
   pauses
even his gestures had commas

in his private workshop
behind a wall of resurrected TV sets
and engine parts
collected from the side of the road
he spent his spare time
polishing granddaddy's old saws
chisels and hammers
reconstructing assorted junk and found objects
into miniature antique furniture
and scale models of his dreams

just piddlin', he'd say
deflecting accusations
of creating something beautiful
no one ever called this man
an artist
no book spine whispers his name
yet every time I open my mouth
I can hear him sing

Born and raised in Danville, Kentucky, **Frank X Walker** was founder and executive director of the Bluegrass Black Arts Consortium, program coordinator of the University of Kentucky's King Cultural Center, and helped direct Purdue University's Black Cultural Center on the way to his current position as writer-in-residence at Northern Kentucky University. Walker, a visual artist, photographer, and writer, is also editor/publisher of *PLUCK! The Journal of Affrilachian Arts & Culture.*

He is the author of four poetry collections—*When Winter Come: The Ascension of York, Black Box, Affrilachia,* and *Buffalo Dance: The Journey of York,* which won the 35th Annual Lillian Smith Book Award—and editor of two collections: *America! What's My Name? The "Other" Poets Unfurl the Flag* and *Eclipsing a Nappy New Millennium.* Among Walker's awards are a Kentucky Arts Council Al Smith Fellowship, the 2006 Thomas D. Clark Literary Award for Excellence, and a $75,000 Lannan Literary Fellowship in poetry. He has lectured, conducted workshops, read poetry, and exhibited at more than three hundred national conferences and universities in the United States, Ireland, and Cuba.

Walker has appeared on television in PBS's GED Connection Series titled *Writing: Getting Ideas on Paper,* appeared in *In Performance at the Governor's Mansion,* and in *Living the Story: The Civil Rights Movement in Kentucky.* He also coproduced a video documentary, *Coal Black Voices: The History of the Affrilachian Poets,* which won the 2002–2003 Jesse Stuart Award presented by the Kentucky School Media Association. "As a cofounder of the Affrilachian Poets and the creator of the word 'Affrilachia,' I believe it is my responsibility to say as loudly and often as possible that people and artists of color are part of the past and present of the multistate Appalachian region extending from northern Mississippi to southern New York," Walker says. "As a writer, I choose to focus on social justice issues as well as multiple themes of family, identity and place."

On "Beacon": "I wrote this poem to bring attention to one of the many significant Kentucky African Americans who are part of the state's history but often overlooked. Millions of tourists have visited Mammoth Cave without appreciating the role enslaved African Americans played in its history. Whenever I can sneak an important history lesson into a poem, I count it as a victory."

LYNNELL
Edwards

b. 1965

And Mathew Brady Photographing It All

How those first photographs stun them
In New York, battlefields wrecked
With bodies bloated and still as fish, eyes white,
Screwed toward the preponderance of sky.
Every horizon low in the frame, every border
Bleeds to the edge. This the war that started
As a fray on a grassy hill, a few shots volleyed across
Calm water, a local action easily patched.
But now here it is, chromatic, huge, hanging
At eye level, piled against the warehouse walls.
The photos overfill the gallery, spill into the papers
Where mothers see their moon-faced boys for the first time
Among the dead, stacked and charred like timber,
Strewn like dolls against a sand embankment,
Bandaged and slumped across a cannon.
Now the lists of the dead grow longer. Now the shutters
Click at will in the camps where Brady's men
Roam unchecked. Now the lens widens to embrace
the apocalypse of Shiloh, the terror of Antietam,
"The Hornet's Nest," "The Slaughter Pen,"
"The Harvest of Death," "The Devil's Den."
Just a little more light, just a little more speed
Now, and he will frame the shot, the fall
The ascendance into heaven that gives us
Something for our papers, something for our pain.

The Baby Plays Monopoly

Rain again on the second day, and the tattered
boxes are unshelved, hauled into
the center room for children to abuse.
They grab Monopoly, squabble for
the top hat, yacht, old shoe, train, initiate
the barter for Railroads, Park Place, *trade for*
all the Reds. Beyond the din adults relax and sigh
with newspapers, coffee, review the weather
signs, consider dinner plans, and someone
turns the baby loose, sets it babbling,
spitting into motion, spastic at their feet,
unseen now advancing toward the knot
of cousins tossing dice, their lullaby
of chatter, the flutter of their nimble hands.
And now the baby lurches huge beside
the game, its globe-like head bobbing, pushing
to their huddle. A blunt knee covers Jail;
one hand like a spatula flips a tiny,
gabled house. Another like Godzilla
smashes *GO*, and still the baby keeps
on coming. The brother lugs the baby sack-like
off the board, drops it squirming by
the chair. But the baby bleats and rights
itself, returns in greater force, scatters
Chance, flattens stacks of cash. A sister
tries confining it behind a desk,
distracts it with some plastic keys, but baby
will not relent, louder in its angry
squall, clever in its progress, until
the baby now sits flailing at the center

of the game, insisting in its right
to be the baby, the owner of all properties,
the arbiter of wealth, the last great family
tycoon making all the rules, chewing
up the fragile sibling contracts in its toothless
baby mouth, compounding all the debt
in its ferocious baby fists.

from "Alabama Interlude"

All I Know about Love

for JME

Let's take off those pants and get into the box of reptiles!
—Joe Rogan, host of *Fear Factor: All-Female Version*

And it must start, somehow
with reptiles. And women
wearing pansy-colored
halter tops, taking off
their pants and squealing,
whether with delight
or fear the casual viewer
cannot tell, but must
himself decide which babe
can earn the most points,
by retrieving the most
gold coins from the bottom
of the reptile box.

Son, a good woman will
not take off her pants
because you ask, will not
auction her shame
for shiny objects,
will not bite
the first sweet fruit
you dangle at her lips.

And though I cannot
save you from
the angle of hips

slipping forward,
the slope of a shoulder
under moonlight,
a tangle of hair
spooling like silk
through your hands,

all I know about love
does not contain
a reptile box, race
toward reward, points
awarded the last one standing.

And what slight difference
you will someday divine
between fear and delight,
hold tight when the world
cracks open, shows its black box
of desire, its treasure
of petal, earth, bright fang.

For You, October's Boy

And now and then a solitary boy
Journeying and muttering o'er his dreams of joy
—John Clare, "October"

All the late dahlias lighting the yard,
and the round-hipped roses, fragrant and dark;
the flash of chrysanthemums in every pot;
vegetable gardens still green and stalked.

A startled deer across the path; a rush
of ground pheasants by your footfall flushed;
sweep of owls' wings; the calling nightingale;
Libra weighing the moon in her star-tipped scales.

And for you too, morning's witness:
first cry of light igniting white fields,
tufted fog spilling into furrows and ditches;
the ascendant sun, the imminent blue; and see,
the woman you love stepping forward,
impossible harvest balanced at her hip.

A native Kentuckian, **Lynnell Edwards** has published two books of poetry —*The Highwayman's Wife* and *The Farmer's Daughter.* Her reviews and essays have appeared in such magazines and journals as the *Georgia Review* and *Professions,* and her short fiction in *New Madrid* and *Pearl.* She has also written a stage adaptation of Charlotte Perkins Gilman's "The Yellow Wallpaper," which was performed at Concordia University in Portland, Oregon. Now living in Louisville, Edwards has published scholarly articles in *Composition Studies* and the *Georgia Review.*

The daughter of an academic dean (her mother) and a cattle and tobacco farmer, she grew up in a "very literate household where reading and writing were virtues and actively in practice." After moving to Portland with her mother and brother when she was in high school, Edwards returned to Kentucky for college and graduate school but then moved back to Oregon and lived there from 1994 to 2005. "I think being away from Kentucky gave me a really interesting perspective and appreciation for certain aspects of the landscape and culture. Some of my newest work reflects this connection, and I think there's a strong regional theme in my new, third manuscript."

Edwards's Kentucky roots are deep. After earning a bachelor's degree from Centre College in Danville, she completed an M.A. in English and a Ph.D. in rhetoric and composition from the University of Louisville. Her poetry has been recognized by an Al Smith Fellowship from the Kentucky Arts Council.

On "All I Know about Love": "Both my boys really liked *Fear Factor,* the stunt-dare reality game show from which the epigraph for the poem comes. This poem emerged almost immediately after I heard the host utter these words: 'Let's take off those pants and get into the box of reptiles!' When I looked up, I saw that my youngest son (then in fifth grade) was watching some all-female version of the show where the assembled contestants were being asked to do exactly that. Instead of being a proactive mother and switching the channel or explaining how this was not really appropriate, I slunk off to write the poem. What I like about the way it turned out is how the idiom of the show itself—'which babe,' 'reptile box,' 'halter tops'—swerves into a more formally sensual and finally highly symbolic language."

MAURICE
Manning

b. 1966

Sleeping in the Wilderness

No matter how well you dress the hide
a buffalo rug will always smell like buffalo:
it is a rank odor and wild, charged with old
glands and cud and the memory of running ten
winters, the last two blind. So you take your bed
in this way, raking dry leaves into a grave-sized
mound beneath you, pulling the mossy cloak
upon you and you spit out the last bitter cinders
from your fire and submerge your head, feeling
the dank fur on your face. And you try to breathe.
What good are the dim stars on such nights?
They only make heaven seem colder and farther
away. So you rekindle the dream about Rebecca,
in which the two of you are resting in the shade
of a sycamore and you skip a rock for her across
the river, and as you prepare to skip another,
she grabs your rough hand and puts it in her hair.
Then she lays her generous bones next to yours.
In the morning, you wrap the rug around you,
check your powder, rub some ashes on your teeth
and go to the creek where you wash all traces of night
from your face. You walk until walking warms you,
then you fold the rug and lash it to your horse
and you keep going to the next blue lick and the next,
the taste of salt already on your tongue, a precious
grain of civilization clinging to your brutal frame
like a pocket watch or a lock of hair; but you are looking
for an elk, or a bear, sniffing the air for musk.

"D. Boon Kilt Bar on This Tree, 1760"

It's true, I've had my trouble spelling easy words
like *bear*, though I've killed one with my bare hands;
and some men would have felt this was a feat
worth writing down, as proof of manliness,
but that is not my carving: history has
painted me as prideful. Another fact:
I took a Shawnee squaw in the winter of 1770.
I was cold and she was warm—much better than
a dreary cave was her fair lodge; she soothed
me with her sweet Algonquian voice. I never
told Rebecca and it was not a difficult secret
to keep. You cannot blame a man for keeping
warm. Besides, Rebecca lay once with my brother,
Ned, which I understood, one Boone being good
as any other. I was much obliged to that long-legged
Shawnee girl and left her the hides of two deer
for her troubles. The kindness of those days is not
recorded. We thought less of sin than one may think.

Wabete's Season

I never shot an elk in rut.
If he were making marks on trees,
removing antler felt, or curling
his upper lip to better sniff
the air, I let him be. I loved
to see one blow and shake the ground
with his desire. The fire alive
in him, the season of his fearless strut,
his yearly wound, would soon compel
my hands to drop and gently rest
my rifle on my shoulder. Keen
on making mothers, he would bound
away. I'd hear him bellow from
a farther ridge, announcing himself,
as though he were a king who needed
no entourage or introduction;
I'd smile and leave him to his pleasure.

The Pleasure of Stasis

I wasn't always moving through the woods:
some days I sat like feldspar in a rock
fast bound to the world around me, or a wick
in wax, a candle's only vein, whose task
is waiting for a flame. But do we need
to burn to find contentment? Is life all light
and motion, or is there room for shadows, dim
and slow, retreating only when the earth
decides to creak a few lazy degrees
around on its hinge—as a woman clicks her teeth
in mild disgust and pulls the shawl from her lap,
confessing that the fire is enough—the earth
moves in two directions, like a gate
swinging open and closed with the pulse of the wind.
The fixed point must be the throne of life,
the regal seat between an ash and anvil,
reluctance and zeal. My point is we cannot
chase light alone; we must go back and forth.
One night a bear approached my camp
and I lay still and let him sniff my bones;
his nose against my neck was like the taste
of freedom; he took his paw and rolled me
over, as if I were a rotten log
and underneath a treasure chest of bugs.

Envoy

Man who believes television
is the mouthpiece of the devil,
seeks female with similar views.

Attention all ladies who like
biscuits: man has gristmill
and two or three acres of wheat.

Are you a woman cast out from society?
Man with thirty-seven acres
and big muscles can provide refuge.

Would like to find sober woman (beer okay),
interested in pick-up trucks, old-time
Gospel music, buffalo trails.

Grown man who likes red dogs
and skipping rocks, hoping against
hope some woman likes same.

Man who lives several hundred
years in the past would like to find
woman zealous for spinning wheels.

Eccentric (?) gentleman (negotiable)—
tinker/farmer searching the heavens
for the true spark of love (breast-size unimportant). Please.

Kentucky native **Maurice Manning** has published three books of poetry—
*Bucolics; A Companion for Owls, Being the Commonplace Book of D.
Boone, Long Hunter, Back Woodsman, &c.;* and *Lawrence Booth's Book
of Visions,* which won the Yale Younger Poets Prize in 2000. Both *Bucolics*
and *A Companion for Owls* made the Booksense (American Booksellers
Association) Poetry Top Ten List, and *A Companion for Owls* was also
named Best Collection of Poetry in 2004 by the Southeast Booksellers
Association.

Manning holds an M.F.A. degree in creative writing from the University
of Alabama. He is currently a professor of English at Indiana University
and works in the Warren Wilson M.F.A. Program for Writers. His poems,
articles, and reviews have appeared in dozens of magazines and journals,
including *Poetry,* the *Southern Review,* the *Yale Review,* the *Virginia
Quarterly Review,* and the *New Yorker.*

Some of the locals he met in his first jobs in Danville, Kentucky, had an
immense influence on Manning's writing and thinking. "For a while I was
the shoeshine boy at the barber shop. Then I had a paper route, and later
in high school I worked at the hardware store. Such experiences often put
me face-to-face with some of Danville's local characters, old-timers and
eccentrics. I was aware even then that I was getting an important and
unique education—old men telling stories in barber shops and hardware
stores—and I was always eager to listen. That's the kind of literature I
grew up with—I listened to it and loved it."

In college Manning began reading the Romantic poets and felt a strong
kinship with them. He adds, "I also fell in love with poetry in general, as a
potent means of expression and as a way of thinking." Manning says he's
always been interested in where poetry comes from, its roots, and has
recently been focusing on the medieval troubadours, "those poets consid-
ered to be the inventors of lyric poetry." Manning cites Wendell Berry and
James Baker Hall as major influences on his work.

On "Sleeping in the Wilderness": "At some point in my research for
A Companion for Owls, it dawned on me how much time Boone spent
utterly alone. For months and months he might not see another human
being. Part of me envies that, but I also realize how easy it is to romanti-
cize the kind of freedom and independence we imagine Boone might have
had. The reality is, he probably got lonely; he probably missed his wife
Rebecca. There might have been days when he was weary from hunting,
weary of the life he lived. That kind of ambivalence is what I tried to cap-
ture in this poem. I think it makes Boone more complicated and honest,
more human and less mythic; and therefore, in some ways, more like us."

DAVIS
McCombs

b. 1969

Tours

The services of a guide cannot, as a rule,
be dispensed with; we alone can disentangle
the winding passageways. I will admit
the tours for me grow burdensome.
How long must I endure their need to fill
with talk the natural silence? I have heard
it all before, their proposed improvements:
Widen the trails so that two carriages
may pass abreast . . . here, a capacious ballroom.
Mere fancies. And yet beneath their words
I have discerned a kind of rough-hewn fear.
From drawing rooms and formal gardens
they come to me, from sunlit lives they enter
the chill, grand and instantaneous night.

Dismantling the Cave Gate

It started with the clang of plates and girders,
one last click of the rusted turnstile,
and then a river of breath had come loose
into the night. The workmen claim it took
the hats from their heads, blew out their lights,
and for a moment they had stood in darkness,
listening to the cave's unearthly moan.
It was a sound not heard in over fifty years
that rippled out into the undergrowth,
whistled across the limestone lintel, and rose—
a rustling, vast and unfamiliar to the bats
beneath the streetlamps and underpasses,
who gathered it in their ears and followed,
dark and fluttering, to the fluttering dark.

Stephen Bishop's Grave

It took four summers here for me to realize
the cave looped back under the Old Guide
Cemetery, that what was mortal floated
in a crust of brittle sandstone or leaked
into the darkest rivers and was caving still.
I went that drizzling night to stand
where the paper-trail he left had vanished:
woodsmoke, mist, a mossed-over name.
I knew enough by then to know that he,
of all people, would prefer the company of rain
to my own, but I went anyway, thinking
of my pale inventions, and stood a long time,
vigilant for his shadow in my own,
his voice as it differed from the wind.

Cave Mummies

Their faces will remain lost in the shadows
of the dry cane-reeds they lit and held aloft.
What comes down to us is mortal, dust—
their intact hair and fingernails, their teeth
worn to the gums by mussels full of sand.
We've probed their last meals matted in their guts
and joined a history of side-show men
who blurred into the archaeologists I've met.
They bend like surgeons in the lantern's light,
but do they ever stop, I've wondered, stare out
into the dark, and ask what brought us here,
all of us, what artifact will tell the future
of a longing wild and inarticulate,
of a dark place loved and gotten in the blood?

Born in Louisville, **Davis McCombs** grew up in Hart County, Kentucky, in a small community called Woodsonville, twelve miles from Mammoth Cave National Park. His family lived in a house built by his great-great grandfather nearly two hundred years ago.

Currently a professor of English and director of the writing program at the University of Arkansas, McCombs has published two books of poems, *Ultima Thule,* which won the Yale Younger Poets Award in 2000, and *Dismal Rock,* which was named 2007 Kentucky Book of the Year in Poetry by the Southern Kentucky Book Fest. His many other awards include an Individual Artist Fellowship from the Arkansas Arts Council, a Ruth Lilly Poetry Fellowship, a Stegner Fellowship at Stanford University, and a grant from the National Endowment for the Arts.

McCombs's poems have appeared in *Poetry,* the *Missouri Review,* the *Kenyon Review, Virginia Quarterly Review,* and *The Best American Poetry 2008*. He has been featured on National Public Radio's *Morning Edition* with Bob Edwards and CBS radio's *The Osgood File.*

McCombs's nearly eight years working as a park ranger at Mammoth Cave National Park continues to provide the raw material for his poetry. "I write about Kentucky—specifically, the beautiful Caveland or Cave Country where I grew up—almost exclusively," he says. "When people ask me what I'm working on now, I say that I'm writing the third installment of my long, three-book love letter to South Central Kentucky." And the writers he says he's most drawn to—Wendell Berry, Richard Taylor, Aleda Shirley, Jeffrey Skinner, and Bobbie Ann Mason—are, he admits, "a very Kentucky crowd."

On "Dismantling the Cave Gate": "I wrote an early draft of this poem while reading Faulkner's *Light in August*. To say that Faulkner's style worked its way into that draft would be to understate the case. The poem at that stage was two pages long and composed of sentences so complex and endless that they ended up collapsing under their own weight. When I went back to this draft a year later, I ruthlessly cut and slashed and hammered the poem into its present fourteen lines in an attempt to banish the Faulknerian echoes. And you know what? I still hear Faulkner in there. That style of his—it's addictive, insidious."

POEM CREDITS

Berry, Wendell. "The Man Born to Farming," "Rising," "Her First Calf," and "The Peace of Wild Things" from *Collected Poems, 1957–1982,* San Francisco: North Point Press, 1985. "Burley Coulter's Song for Kate Helen Branch," "III Look Out" and "VI" (from *Sabbaths 2003*) from *Given: New Poems,* Washington, D.C.: Shoemaker & Hoard, 2005. "Come Forth," "To the Unseeable Animal," "Three Elegiac Poems," and "Testament" from *The Selected Poems of Wendell Berry,* Washington, D.C.: Counterpoint, 1998.

Boes, Don. "Feature Race" and "Reunion" from *The Eighth Continent,* Boston: Northeastern University Press, 1993. "Paving Kentucky" and "For Charles Mingus (1922–1979)" from *Railroad Crossing,* Georgetown, Ky.: Finishing Line Press, 2005.

Crunk, Tony. "Elders" from *Cumberland,* Birmingham, Ala.: Mercy Seat Press, 2007. "Visiting the Site of One of the First Churches My Grandfather Pastored," "Souvenirs," and "After Visiting Home for Christmas" from *Living in the Resurrection,* New Haven, Conn.: Yale University Press, 1995.

Driskell, Kathleen. "Optometrist's Visit" from *Laughing Sickness,* Louisville: Fleur-de-lis Press, 1999. "Why I Mother You the Way I Do," "With a Shiner, My Husband Enters the Flower Shop," and "To the Outdoor Wedding" from *Seed across Snow,* Granada Hills, Calif.: Red Hen Press, 2009.

Edwards, Lynnell. "And Mathew Brady Photographing It All," "The Baby Plays Monopoly," "All I Know about Love," and "For You, October's Boy" from *The Highwayman's Wife,* Granada Hills, Calif.: Red Hen Press, 2007.

Finney, Nikky. "Black Orion" from *Rice,* Toronto: Sister Vision Press, 1995. "Sex," "The New Cotton," and "The Making of Paper" from *The World Is Round,* Atlanta: InnerLight Publishing, 2003.

Garland, Max. "Hold on Me" from *Hunger Wide as Heaven,* Cleveland: Cleveland State University Poetry Center, 2006. "Requiem for a Boom Town," "The Termite Confessions," and "For a Johnson County Snowfall" from *The Postal Confessions,* Amherst, Mass.: University of Massachusetts Press, 1995.

Gentry, Jane. "A Garden in Kentucky" and "In the Moment of My Death: For My Father" from *A Garden in Kentucky: Poems,* Baton Rouge: Louisiana State University Press, 1995. "Taking the Train from Maysville to New York," "Hunting for a Christmas Tree after Dark," "Penelope's Night Out," and "Their Bed" from *Portrait of the Artist as a White Pig: Poems,* Baton Rouge: Louisiana State University Press, 2006.

Gorham, Sarah. "Sickle Billed Hummingbird" and "I Go Back" from *Don't Go Back to Sleep,* Sparks, Md.: Galileo Press, 1989. "Late Evening Love Poem" and "Honeymoon, Pleasant Hill" from *The Cure,* New York: Four Way Books, 2003.

Greene, Jonathan. "The Ideal Reader" from *Idylls,* Rocky Mount, N.C.: North Carolina College Press, 1983. "Mao" from *Idylls,* Rocky Mount, N.C.: North Carolina College Press, 1990. "Scarecrow Poems" from *Of Moment,* Frankfort, Ky.: Gnomon Press, 1998. "Recollections of Bass Rhythms of Hip-Hop Heard from a Distant Van" and "Waiting" from *Fault Lines,* Frankfort, Ky.: Broadstone Books, 2004.

Hall, James Baker. "Item One in a General Theory of Things," "It Felt So Good but Many Times I Cried," "The Buffalo," "Welcoming the Season's First Insects," "Ridge Owl Black Dog," and "For Mary Ann" from *The Total Light Process: New and Selected Poems,* Lexington: University Press of Kentucky, 2004.

Hurlow, Marcia. "Aliens Are Intercepting My Brain Waves" and "The Pantheist Who Loved His Wife" from *Aliens Are Intercepting My Brain Waves,* Brockport, N.Y.: State Street Press, 1991. "Margin of Loss," "The Sisterhood," and "The Music of the Spiders" from *Anomie,* Cincinnati: WordTech Communications, 2004.

Kendrick, Leatha. "Refusing a Spinal" from *Heart Cake,* Aldeborough, England: Sow's Ear Press, 2000. "Wedding Album," "Second Opinion," "Costume. Fakery. The Sell.," and "In Passing" from *Second Opinion,* Cincinnati: WordTech Communications, 2008.

Lyon, George Ella. "My Grandfather in Search of Moonshine," "Mother's Day at the Air Force Museum," and "Salvation" from *Catalpa,* Nicholasville, Ky.: Wind Publications, 2007. "Catechisms" from *Where I'm From,* New York: Absey & Company, 1999.

Manning, Maurice. "Envoy" from *Lawrence Booth's Book of Visions,* New Haven, Conn.: Yale University Press, 2001. "Sleeping in the Wilderness," "'D. Boon Kilt Bar on This Tree, 1760,'" "Wabete's Season," and "The Pleasure of Stasis" from *A Companion for Owls,* Orlando, Fla.: Harcourt, 2004.

McCombs, Davis. "Tours," "Dismantling the Cave Gate," "Stephen Bishop's Grave," and "Cave Mummies" from *Ultima Thule,* New Haven, Conn.: Yale University Press, 2000.

Shipley, Vivian. "With My Father outside the West Wing of Hospice" and "First Ice" from *Gleanings,* Hammond: Louisiana Literature Press, 2003. "Corner of Bellefonte and Heather Way, Lexington, Kentucky" from *Down of Hawk,* Aldeborough, England: Sow's Ear Press, 2001. "Coma: Bachus Hospital, Norwich, Connecticut" from *Hardboot,* Hammond: Louisiana Literature Press, 2005.

Shirley, Aleda. "My Parents When They Were Young," "One Summer Night," and "Hostage to Fortune" from *Chinese Architecture,* Athens, Ga.: University of Georgia Press, 1986. "The Star's Etruscan Argument" from *Dark Familiar,* Louisville: Sarabande Books, 2006.

Skinner, Jeffrey. "Hey Nineteen" and "Uncle Joe" from *A Guide to Forgetting,* Saint Paul, Minn.: Graywolf Press, 1988. "The School of Continuing Education" and "Prodigal" from *Gender Studies,* Oxford, Ohio: Miami University Press, 2002. "Hard Labor" from *Salt Water Amnesia,* Keene, N.Y.: Ausable Press, 2005.

Smock, Frederick. "Heron" and "Homeward" from *Sonnets*, Georgetown, Ky.: Finishing Line Press, 2006. "Poem for Cassius Clay" and "On the Gold Medal That Lies at the Bottom of the Ohio River" from *Gardencourt,* Monterey, Ky.: Larkspur Press, 1997.

St. Clair, Philip. "Menace from Space," "Last Night," "Society," and "Into the Wires" from *Human Landscapes: Three Books of Poems,* Huron, Ohio: Bottom Dog Press, 1997.

Survant, Joe. "Anne Waters, December 28, 1842," "Anne Waters, December 21, 1862," "Alpheus Waters, February 20, 1863," "Alpheus Waters, July 13, 1882," and "Anne Waters, September 7, 1882" from *Anne & Alpheus, 1842–1882,* Fayetteville: University of Arkansas Press, 1996. "At the Camp Meeting" from *Rafting Rise,* Gainesville: University Press of Florida, 2002.

Taylor, Richard. "On Whapping My Index Finger with a Roofing Hammer" and "The Lava Beds at Pompeii" from *In the Country of Morning Calm,* Monterey, Ky.: Larkspur Press, 1998. "An Inner Tour of Shaker Village at Pleasant Hill, Kentucky" and "Notes for a Manual on Form" from *Stone Eye,* Monterey, Ky.: Larkspur Press, 2001. "Imagining My Own Death" and "Water Hauling on Sunday Morning" from *Braintree,* Louisville: Scienter Press, 2004.

Walker, Frank X. "God's House," "Promises," and "Revisionist History" from *Buffalo Dance: The Journey of York,* Lexington: University Press of Kentucky, 2004. "Praise Song" from *When Winter Come: The Ascension of York,* Lexington: University Press of Kentucky, 2008. "Beacon" and "Last Words" from *Black Box,* Lexington, Ky.: Old Cove Press, 2005.

Worley, Jeff. "Sleeping with Two Women," "Playing Possum," and "His Funeral" from *Happy Hour at the Two Keys Tavern,* Minneapolis: Mid-List Press, 2006. "On My Deathbed" from *The Only Time There Is,* Minneapolis: Mid-List Press, 1995.

PHOTO CREDITS

James Baker Hall (Wendell Berry, p. 9); Gaby Bedetti (Don Boes, p. 212); Maria Morrison (Tony Crunk, p. 189); Terry Driskell (Kathleen Driskell, p. 219); John Nation (Lynnell Edwards, p. 240); Brad Luttrell/*Kentucky Kernel* (Nikky Finney, p. 198); Pilar Gómez-Ibáñez (Max Garland, p. 145); Tim Collins (Jane Gentry, p. 45); Laura Skinner (Sarah Gorham, p. 181); Dobree Adams (Jonathan Greene, p. 81); Rebecca Gayle Howell (James Baker Hall, p. 31); Jennifer Mattox (Marcia Hurlow, p. 154); Ann Olson (Leatha Kendrick, p. 136); Ann W. Olson (George Ella Lyon, p. 127); Steve Cody (Maurice Manning, p. 248); Russell Cothren (Davis McCombs, p. 255); Isabel Chenoweth (Vivian Shipley, p. 88); Michael McBride (Aleda Shirley, p. 171); Laura Skinner (Jeffrey Skinner, p. 117); Olga-Maria Cruz (Frederick Smock, p. 164); Christina St. Clair (Philip St. Clair, p. 97); Dwight Pounds (Joe Survant, p. 66); Tracy Hawkins (Frank X Walker, p. 229); Frank Stephenson (Jeff Worley, p. 106).

INDEX OF TITLES AND FIRST LINES

Titles are shown in *italic* type.